THE LIVING
LEADER

PENNY FERGUSON

THE LIVING
LEADER

**BECOME THE LEADER
YOU WANT TO BE**

Copyright © The Infinite Ideas Company Limited, 2006
The right of Penny Ferguson to be identified as the author of this book
has been asserted in accordance with the Copyright, Designs and
Patents Act 1988

First published in 2006 by
The Infinite Ideas Company Limited
36 St Giles
Oxford, OX1 3LD
United Kingdom
www.infideas.com

Reprinted 2007, 2008, 2010, 2013, 2014, 2015

A CIP catalogue record for this book is available from the British
Library

ISBN   978-1-904902-89-8

Brand and product names are trademarks or registered trademarks of
their respective owners.

Designed and typeset by Sparks – www.sparkspublishing.com
Cover designed by Cylinder
Printed in Great Britain

MIX
Paper from
responsible sources
FSC   FSC® C013056
www.fsc.org

CONTENTS

ACKNOWLEDGEMENTS

This is a joy for me to do because it enables me to thank publicly some of the many people who have impacted my life – to give them the recognition they deserve. Firstly, Richard Burton – a publisher with courage. From the moment we met, you supported and encouraged me, and helped me find the belief that I can write! John Duggan – you have read and reread all of this book with such care and attention and it has come alive as a result of your outstanding editing. Thank you so much.

Once again, my clients inspire me and take me to new levels of learning; sometimes I wonder if they know how much they stretch me! I feel privileged to work with so many wonderful people. Amongst this amazing group there are some that I would especially like to thank. Chris Weston – you are such a wonderful example of how great the difference can be when you lead in this way; your passion and caring for people shines through in all that you do. The results you achieved in BGB, then BGS and now what you are doing in Direct Energy speak for themselves; thank you for taking the time to write about your thoughts on leadership for me. Paul Stobart – you are a wonderful leader and it was so very good to know through the Marketing Hall of Legends that you demonstrate all that we teach – you inspired them! Ewan McCulloch, you are simply amazing and I believe that you embody all that I talk about – working with you is a sheer delight. Steve Back – what would I do without you in my life? I hope I never have to find out. To all of the people I have mentioned above, it is very special that you have welcomed me into your lives, not just as a consultant but as a friend – I feel truly lucky.

For my friends and colleagues, I hardly know where to begin and couldn't possibly name you all – I feel inspired, uplifted and so very supported by you all. A big thank you to everyone in the office who does their best to manage me – a trying task! I have to mention Julia by name – you are without question the very best PA that I have ever had. My life is easier for having you support and challenge me. Also Kath, my wonderful Head of Finance – I cannot imagine anyone showing greater integrity, support and loyalty than you have to me over the past ten years. I would not be where I am today if I had not had you beside me.

So, too, all our wonderful associates who deliver programmes with such passion and courage! Tasha – you have known me, worked with me, been a friend for many, many years and are now truly an expert at spreading these messages with your fantastic delivery of our leadership programmes. Trish, the trauma and challenges you have had to face in the last couple of years would have crushed most people, but the way that you have come through them, still as a wonderful colleague, trainer and friend is amazing. You inspire me and I love you dearly. Karen – I hope you know how much it means to me to have you working so closely with the company now, and even more so to have you as a much loved friend. Kirsten – you give so much of your life, your friendship and your love and it is reciprocated and valued more than you can imagine. Pat Lee – thank you for your belief in me and for your incredible determination to do the best for each individual in every part of your life. You epitomise a giving, caring and inspirational leader and I feel very privileged to now have you as part of the team. Angus it was fantastic to have you first as a client and now as a colleague. Thank you for joining us. Tim and Mandy Paine – having bought our offices from you I had no idea what an impact you would have in helping to get me into the movies! We would all be struggling with many of our programmes without your help, guidance and considerable expertise. You even make me look quite good occasionally! You are now a very special and integral part of my life and were there through some of the worst times as well as the best: even if I am concerned that I may become a cruisaholic! Thank you from the bottom of my heart.

A big 'thank you' and a huge amount of love to my children James, Philip, Richard, Lucy, Emma and Mark. You all, in your different ways, have given and continue to give me the greatest leadership challenges (some more so than others!), which means that you are also my most powerful teachers. You give me so much love and care in many different ways. I am proud to be your mother and love you all so very much. I am highly delighted that you have brought me some truly delicious grandchildren who are a complete delight and give me so much pleasure. There will come a time when I actually am able to spend more time with them. I am so in awe of you as parents – you demonstrate all the things that I teach and so abysmally failed to do much of the time when I was raising you. I am ecstatic that you, Emma, have decided to come back and join me in the company – it is quite wonderful for me and I see you growing into the role every day. I hope you know how immensely proud of you I am and look forward to you taking over!

And finally I dedicate this book to two amazing and wonderful people. Sherilyn Shackell – you came into my life at a fortuitous time. You inspire me, challenge me to bring out the best in myself, listen to me when I need an ear, encourage me when I am worried, push me to think differently and care for me always. You are a wonderful lady, a special friend and one of the best things that has happened to me. Christine Mansfield – there are not enough words to describe how supportive you have been to me over the many years since we met. You so often rearrange your life to help me when I need it, you are an incredibly valuable asset to the business, you stretch yourself in so many different ways when I need your help, you lift me when I am down and laugh with me in the good times. Your friendship and caring mean so very much to me and you are one of the most thoughtful, giving and caring people that I have ever been lucky enough to have come into my life. To both of you – this book only came into existence because of your encouragement, help and guidance. You are both inspirational leaders and I love and admire you so much. Thank you from the bottom of my heart.

FOREWORD

Leadership is a difficult but essential element in any venture. It is talked about widely and there are many different forms, but in its most effective form it is rare in business. Too often the trappings of success, hierarchy and ego get in the way of truly effective leadership. It is not easy to get right, but at its best will allow the creation of teams that perform and organisations that deliver and thrive beyond any individual.

Leadership has a number of elements: setting direction, prioritisation, injecting a sense of urgency and energy; I'm sure there are many more, but at the heart of it are the people a leader has the privilege to lead: building their confidence so they can achieve more than they ever expected, inspiring them. This is not easy, it is not a science, it requires thought and constant attention. It can be frightening or invigorating and can be achieved in many different ways.

To me it has always been best summed up by Lao Tsu, who said, 'As for the best leaders, the people barely notice their existence; the next best the people honour and praise; the next the people fear; but, when the best leader's work is done, the people say "we did it ourselves".'

Read it carefully and think about it.

I first started to learn consciously about leadership when I went to Sandhurst, where the British army trains its leaders. It is a tough environment, both physically and mentally. Leading soldiers, particularly in times of stress, is a real test of leadership. I remember being very surprised to learn that the motto of the academy is 'Serve to lead'. As an officer you have the right to order a soldier to carry out a particular task. How a soldier does that is vitally important: do they trust you, are they inspired? Having their best interests at heart and building their confidence are both very important in achieving this, so the motto is a good reminder of what is at the heart of leadership. It has stayed with me ever since and is always a useful reminder.

If any leader is to get the best out of a team or an organisation then the ability of the people within that organisation to perform to their utmost, to be confident about what they do, is key; not just for short-term success, but for success that will last. It must outlive any one individual.

This book and the Leadership Development Programme provide a good foundation, or if you have been leading for a while, a good reminder, about leadership. If you can live by these principles I have no doubt that you will end up being a truly effective and powerful leader.

Chris Weston
CEO
Direct Energy

■

I was fortunate enough, several years ago, to attend a leadership programme run by Penny Ferguson. The experience changed my entire perspective on myself, my career and, most importantly, my life. It's not that there's anything necessarily 'new' in the content, indeed many of the models and theories are well established, but it works because leadership theory is brought to life and made to feel personal.

I was so convinced by the programme that I chose to go through the Masterclass to be in a position where I could deliver the learning myself.

This book contains much of the thinking on which the programme is based and I hope you will be inspired to put some of these ideas into practice and experience for yourself the positive impact they can have.

Paul Stobart
CEO Northern Europe
Sage

INTRODUCTION

Making the simple complicated is commonplace; making the complicated simple, awesomely simple, that's creative.

Charles Mingus

My understanding of leadership has changed considerably over the last few years. This has come about both through personal experiences and from working with many amazing individuals and organisations. Until about 12 years ago I believed leadership was about developing the necessary skills and continually acquiring more knowledge around the various theories on the subject. Learning these skills and putting them into practice – however difficult this might be – would ensure success.

Since then, my whole thinking has changed. Learning skills in isolation just doesn't work, and anyway leadership is not primarily about what you do, it is about who you are and who you choose to be. Leadership is more 'being' than 'doing'; more simplicity than complexity.

I discovered this over a period of time. It began when I was working in business with another consultant, who used to run many senior management development programmes. He was an excellent trainer, and I believed at the time that he was one of the best. However, I became concerned when I realised that even though people left the programme saying how brilliant it had been there was a problem. Despite all the words, the reality was that actual changes in behaviour in the workplace were probably less than 20% of what those attending the programmes had committed to. This left me feeling disillusioned and my level of job satisfaction was low. It was also very confusing. How could intelligent senior people recognise the value of changing their behaviour, commit to it and then still not do it? I started to challenge and question what we were doing on the programmes. However, my critical questioning proved unpopular with the boss and I left to start my own journey of exploration.

I developed a programme that combined traditional thinking with an additional dimension – one that offered people a much deeper level of understanding of leadership. Perhaps, more importantly, one that linked many different elements together, but in such a way that it made complete sense and people could see no good reason not to try it. And guess what? The results were extraordinary! I would love to be able to say that I really knew what I was doing when I developed this programme, but I didn't have a clue. People were saying that just two days had changed their life and I didn't know why. It took me over a year, working with some amazing people, to get an understanding of what was happening. It was this journey of discovery that totally reshaped my thinking on leadership.

I will refer throughout this book to 'the programme'. This is a Personal Leadership Programme (PLP) that I developed over ten years ago and, although it has grown and developed organically, the principles remain the same. It is a three day programme – the first two are run consecutively and the third follows two or three weeks later. To date, over twelve thousand people have attended. The results speak for themselves. Throughout this book – and especially in the final chapter, 'The Proof of the Pudding' – you will see the impact that the programme has had on organisations and on individuals. All this, purely by choosing how you want to be at a truly fundamental level, taking 100% responsibility for your choice and then doing very simple things that consistently support this.

This book is a journey through the programme: every chapter builds on the chapter before and takes you forward with an idea about something that you can do differently. Each behaviour change, if put into practice, will have a positive outcome. The book follows a similar path of discovery to the programme.

- *Integral Performance* is an overview of the programme in its entirety. When people arrive, they may want to explore answers to the question: why am I here?
- *Behind the Mask* offers the possibility of getting to know ourselves and others at a deeper level.
- *Accept Responsibility; Leadership is About Me!* These two parts of the programme involve the group discussing a key part of the whole foundation of leadership – what does responsibility really mean?
- *Communicate Responsibly; Getting Everyone Involved.* During the discussion the facilitator observes and measures the communicating behaviour. Agreement is reached about the preferred style of communicating behaviour and the comparable individual measurement is then discussed. Typically there is a significant gap between perception and reality.
- *Leaders Listen; Questions, Questions and more Questions!; Finding the Right Question.* These three parts offer an in-depth look at the importance of certain aspects of communicating and how it is impossible to look at communicating without looking at responsibility – the two are inseparable.
- *Developing the Right People; Flipping the Pyramid – Releasing People Potential.* These two parts ask the vital questions: Have we got the right people and are we truly helping them express their talents and their abilities as leaders?
- *Demonstrating Value.* What are we more inclined to focus on, people's strengths or their weaknesses?

- *What Style of Leadership?* Is there only one style of leadership or are there others that work as well?
- *Where am I Heading?* If you don't know where you are going then any old path will do and that is not how the best leaders think.
- *Living in the Present.* When and where is change possible and what am I now going to do? There is only one place that you can change – and that is in the present moment!
- *Company Culture* draws together the sum of all the parts that makes the organisation that we now work in.
- *The Proof of the Pudding* adds flesh to the bones of theory, illustrating the success of the programme with a detailed look at some case studies.

You can choose to read the book from start to finish as though on a journey or, if you wish, you can just dip in and read a chapter. Try that idea and see what impact it has and then take another dip. This is entirely your choice. Reading this book will give you simple ideas that can make a profound difference – but only if you put them into action!

My life has changed dramatically as a result of all that I have learned. I remember Joseph Jaworski saying in his inspirational book *The Inner Path of Leadership* that for him the pivotal and life changing moment was when his wife told him that she wanted a divorce after 20 years of marriage. For me the pivotal moment was when my son died at the age of 26. I stood back and re-evaluated my life and took a long hard look at where I was right then. I didn't like what I saw very much. I decided enough was enough and in that moment recognised that for everything that happened in my life I was blaming the outside circumstances. However, in every situation there was one common denominator – me!

It was a life choosing moment. My real journey started there and then. In my first book, *Transform your life*, I shared from a very personal perspective the impact that changing my thinking has had on my life. I now share with you the things that I have learned about leadership through working with some very special people. I truly hope that you will get some insights that will enable you to become all that, at some level, you already are. To become the leader that you choose to be.

INTEGRAL PERFORMANCE 1

Leadership is a potent combination of strategy and character.

But if you must be without one, be without the strategy.

Norman Schwarzkopf

An organisation needs a balance between two elements to be successful. Firstly, it needs a very clear vision – where it wants to go with whatever products it wants to sell, how it wants to be seen in the market place, what culture it wants and the strategy of how it intends getting there. Secondly, in order to make this a reality, an organisation needs individuals who have the right skills and attitude to be able to deliver what is required in line with the vision.

The knack then is to get the balance between the organisation and the individual. Given the complexities of any organisation in today's dynamic and competitive business world, there is a tendency to cover every eventuality with yet another management tool or system. For example, the organisation will want to have plenty of measurement systems in place to make sure that they are delivering what needs to be delivered in line with the priorities that are stated. They will want to know that the results that are committed to are being achieved, that individuals are achieving in line with their agreed goals. On the other side, the individuals will be saying, 'give me the information that I need, give me the resources and training that I require, tell me clearly what the strategy and priorities are and then give me the freedom to get on and do the job you are paying me to do.' Now, assuming that the vision is right in the first place and you have chosen the right people, if this balance could be kept consistently in place, then it would be impossible not to have a high performing organisation.

One organisation that I know well was losing significant amounts of money and decided it needed to change the structure and the way it operated. The management team spent a vast amount on downsizing and completely restructuring the organisation. They brought 'road shows' to all the remaining employees around the country, selling the wonderful new opportunities and the different ways that they were going to be working. It was clearly stated that if everyone was totally committed, they could turn the company around. They put in lots of initiatives that they believed would drive people to work in this new streamlined way and explained the way the new relationships would need to be developed. Then, they sat back and waited for the improved results. What they had done was put all the attention into the organisation box, believing that the new initiatives and systems would compel people to behave differently. They paid little attention to the individual box when the reality was that systems and initiatives alone were not enough. Most of the workforce understood the need for change and what was required of them but, at an emotional level, it was very different. Many felt insecure, and afraid that getting things wrong might have dire consequences. It seemed safer to hold on to doing things that they knew they were good at and doing them the way they had before. No allowance had been made by management for support at the individual level, even though successful change could only come about if people could significantly shift the way they were thinking and then begin to understand and take responsibility at a fundamentally different level.

So why, if it seems this obvious, are so many organisations still not delivering the performance that they really want to? Why do they have to restructure, downsize, change the systems, and so on? Because frequently the wrong area is addressed. The problem is on the individual side but the response is to treat the systems' side.

To give an example, an organisation discovers it has a communication problem. Typically, when there are enough people saying there is a problem, the response is to call in consultants at huge expense. The consultants come in and dig around the bowels of the organisation, write up a fabulous report, which they give to the people at the top. They tell the executive: 'Yes, there is a communication problem, but guess what? We can fix it.' They then come in and spend some time working with many people in the company and, while they are *in situ*, there may well be some change. Ask anyone six months down stream what has changed, however, and I can guarantee you will only get one of two responses. Either 'nothing' or 'not a lot'. I haven't yet worked with any company or top executives who willingly spend money to have something not work. So why does this happen repeatedly? Why do we get into this cyclical nature of fixing?

The issue is on the side of the individual. Each person has the opportunity to take 100% responsibility. If everyone takes full responsibility for communicating, it removes the need to implement a new system to improve things. So, the issue is on the side of the individual and the solution is addressed on the organisation side – no wonder it doesn't last! And not only does it not work, it is not leadership. Leadership is primarily about developing individuals to be the best that they are capable of being and not about putting in systems.

Becoming aware of the language being used and its link to responsibility is a key. One client, with whom we did a lot of work provided a perfect example of how language was enabling everyone to duck responsibility. On each programme that we ran many of the participants told us that they agreed with everything that we were saying and they would love their organisation to succeed in the way we described. However, they felt it would be really difficult because the organisation was so political. Political games were being played all the time. Where were they putting the blame? On the organisation. But, hang on a minute, it is not possible for an organisation to be political, only people can play politics. When we confronted them with the fact that each of them must be playing politics there was a significant degree of discomfort within the group and only after we had run many programmes with people saying similar things did they begin to take responsibility for what was happening. Until they owned the problem, each and every one of them, nothing was going to change. This is also an example of how beliefs drive behaviour. The belief of every person in that room was that communication was an organisational issue and all their actions were then linked to that belief. In allowing them to see it differently, they were able to accept that the belief was invalid and they could take 100% responsibility for beginning to change the games that were being played.

So, your role as a leader is to create the circumstances where the balance is clearly understood and consistently maintained between the organisation and the individual. This is what we mean by 'integral performance'. Please recognise that this is not always an ideal fifty-fifty split. There may be some areas, departments or situations where the balance needs to be flexible and be more one way than the other. There may, for instance, be occasions where members of the finance department are going to be more systems driven and appropriately so, and sales more individually driven, which might also be appropriate. However, please also recognise that too often the temptation is simply to put in a system and expect it alone to solve a problem.

Take, for example, an organisation that embarks on a very large mission to design a product that is critical to the understanding and development of our world. To enable this to happen, the right structures and processes are put in place and the hierarchies and roles that each person needs to fulfil are designated. The timescales are agreed and everyone is committed to the success of the outcome. However, because of the strict adherence to these organisational roles and hierarchies, some of the information that might be critical to the operation is withheld. What now is the outcome likely to be? If vital information is not getting through, then the launch of the product is almost certain to be a failure.

This is precisely what happened in the launches of the space shuttles *Challenger* and *Columbia*, and 14 people died. Here is David L Chandler's article in the *New Scientist* in December 2003/January 2004.

■

Rocket science is not the hard part

The echoes were there almost from the first moment. But as time went on, the striking and sometimes haunting similarities between the tragic endings of the space shuttles Challenger *and* Columbia *only seemed stronger and sadder.*

The sense of déjà vu struck me on the day of the accident, 1 February, during NASA's initial press conference following Columbia*'s break-up high above the south-western US. That was when I first heard that a piece of debris – it later turned out to be foam insulation – had struck the shuttle during its ascent. Anyone who has watched the shuttle's missions over the years knows how fragile and brittle its crucial heat-insulating tiles are. A strike during lift-off* seemed just the kind of thing that might lead to a break-up during re-entry.

Yet NASA managers were dismissive, saying that the strike was almost certainly not the cause of the re-entry accident and that they remained confident in their analysis – which later turned out to be deeply flawed. That reflex denial of the obvious explanation struck a chord. It was just like the aftermath of the Challenger crash in January 1986, when NASA repeatedly insisted that although the launch had taken place in far colder weather than ever before, this was not relevant to the disaster. As we soon discovered, it was crucial. The low temperatures had caused the infamous O-rings to fail to seal the booster rockets, and this led to Challenger's demise. In both cases, as we would later learn, engineers were deeply concerned about these anomalies, but their concerns were never really heard by their managers.

Despite that initial sense of similarity, NASA succeeded for the first week or two after the Columbia crash in persuading the world how much it had changed post-Challenger – how much more open and forthcoming it now was with the facts. And this was a more transparent agency, at least in terms of releasing documents, holding press conferences and trying to answer questions. There was no obvious repeat of blunders such as the immediate firing of a press officer who was too honest in answering a reporter's question. (Might the Challenger astronauts have remained alive until their crew capsule hit the water? Yes, they might.)

But the old NASA surfaced pretty quickly. It became clear from a growing catalogue of missed warning signs that the world's most sophisticated space agency still had not learned the lessons that Richard Feynman and the other members of the Challenger commission had tried to inculcate. Managers were still treating serious anomalies as if they were understood and acceptable, simply because they had not yet caused a catastrophe. It was, as Feynman pointed out, rather like saying Russian roulette is safe just because you have survived the last round.

Former astronaut Sally Ride, who uniquely served on both the Challenger and Columbia investigation boards, wrote a whole chapter in the final report of Columbia describing the strong parallels between the two cases – and the paramount importance of taking heed this time. Aspects of NASA's internal structures, or 'culture' as the Columbia board described it, that caused problems both times were excessively strict adherence to organisational roles and hierarchies, even when critical safety issues were being discussed. Engineers who had concerns about how Challenger's O-rings would work in cold weather did not feel they could say so, just as engineers who were worried about the foam strike, and wanted pictures taken to assess the damage, were stifled in Columbia's management meetings.

The problem is easy to point out, and its role in the loss of both astronaut crews is now clear. But working out how to keep channels of communication open within a huge bureaucracy is still a daunting task.

So daunting, in fact, that one of the greatest minds in modern science considered it a challenge worthy of a life's efforts. I spoke to Richard Feynman a year after the Challenger accident, in what would turn out to be his last press interview, to ask him what he thought had been learned from that investigation. Feynman told me he had become so fascinated by the problem of fostering open communication in a large organisation that if he were starting over, he might study management instead of physics. Even for a mind that *handled concepts of quantum physics as easily as the rest of us order lunch, this was a thorny problem.*

NASA's progress in dealing with the specific technical issues raised in the Columbia *report seems to be on track. But when it comes to fixing its culture, the agency has shown little sign of really addressing the issues.*

This isn't rocket science. Apparently it's harder.

■

This is an extreme case where focus on the 'systems' side of the business caused a tragic outcome. It was all about developing the product, the roles and the structures within the hierarchy and making sure all the procedures were right. Where was the consideration for developing the individuals, making sure that they really had all the information that was needed from every level within the hierarchy? Had the bureaucracy not daunted the engineers or the hierarchy not intimidated them, maybe they would have pushed harder to be heard. In my experience, when you have situations like these it is because of very rigid management structures.

Managers spend much of their time trying to control the circumstances and the outcome, which leads them to drive people to perform at the highest level they can, making certain that everyone is doing it right. This is not leadership. Real leadership is developing the circumstances to ensure all the information is aired, allowing and encouraging people to think for themselves so the highest quality thinking emerges, which then inspires people to find the right way to do it for themselves. The attention is on developing individuals and only putting systems in to support them in doing their job. Not putting the systems and structures in to drive performance. Jim Collins, in his book *Good to Great*, gathers together some fascinating findings and comments from the executives who work in some of the world's great companies. One such finding is that the structures and processes put in place to manage individuals are not seen as critical to success. The attitude is that if someone needs to be managed, then you have the wrong person in the job!

BEHIND THE MASK

To be yourself in a world that is constantly trying to make you something else is the greatest accomplishment.

Ralph Waldo Emerson

As leaders, it is important to develop an ability to know people at a more profound level. When we meet a person for the first time we all make subconscious judgements about who they are, whether or not they have qualities and values that relate to ours, whether or not we are going to get on with them and whether they will do well in our organisation. All this happens within a few seconds of saying hello!

The fact is that we automatically look back in our minds to see how this new person fits in terms of our past relationships and experiences. Imagine for one moment that you grew up in a family where you had an older sister whose friends were always coming round to the house to visit. Amongst them there was a really big girl who, every time she saw you, would tease you mercilessly. When you were very young she used to pull your hair, hide your lunchbox and always be doing things that got you into trouble. As you grew older she grew larger. The teasing transferred itself into more mental games – she constantly wound you up and made derisive remarks about your looks and your achievements. In fact, when she was in your company, she spent the whole time making jokes at your expense and getting all her friends, and even you own sister, to join in and laugh at you.

At some level you're likely to put this down to her size and begin to foster the belief that large women can be bullies. This does not work at a conscious level – it would be so much easier to recognise and deal with if it did – but it impacts at a less visible, subconscious level. You now go to take up your first job in the outside world and you walk into your new office to meet your boss for the first time. In walks a very large woman. The chances are that, without thinking, you will react in a negative way, imagining that this woman is going to be a bully. The likelihood is that you will now behave towards her as though your perception of her is true. Your projection of one personality onto another, and the way you respond to your own thinking, make your imaginings into reality! Of course, she is highly unlikely to be the person you imagine her to be and, over the ensuing months, you begin to realise this and slowly adjust your behaviour. This may take a long time – time that is wasted in terms of you delivering your optimum performance.

Here is another example. Have you ever met someone who, on first meeting, comes across as supremely arrogant? As you dislike arrogance you may avoid this person, make judgements about their comments and feel that you have nothing in common with them. But circumstances force you into a situation where you have to work with them and over the next few weeks, you see a totally different side of them and you begin to realise that this is not arrogance at all. On the contrary, they are painfully shy and have created an image to keep people at a distance because they really don't know how to deal with them.

Both of these are examples of wasted opportunity, where you are prevented from working with people in the most effective way and from helping them step into their full capabilities. Recently, I ran a programme for the top team of a medium sized company. There were four different levels in the hierarchy present, the new chairman, the managing director, the board directors and the regional directors.

In our training, we ask people to introduce themselves in a rather more in-depth way than in the average learning session. We do this whether it is an in-house programme (everyone from the same company and probably even the same team), or an open programme (individuals who are all from different organisations who have never met before). We ask people to answer these questions:

- Who are you? Not just in terms of what you do but in terms of your family, your hobbies, what you feel passionate about.
- What are three things that you feel really good about in your life? For instance, when you wake up in the morning what do you feel good about. It could be a great relationship, a great job or maybe something amazing you have achieved some time ago.
- What is the biggest challenge or opportunity that you are facing in your life right now?
- What are three things that you would really like to get from these two days of training?
- What are three things that you want to give to these first two days?

The trainer always goes first and they will be very open about themselves – who they are and what they are about as a human being. Please note the words that I use here – human being not human doing. Too often, the focus is on what we do rather than who we are. If you have a group of ten people, this can take quite a long time, but it is absolutely vital to the success of the workshop. It forms the foundation from which all learning can grow.

■

No amount of human having or human doing can make up for a deficit in human being.

John Adams

■

At the end of the rather unusual and in-depth introductions and the first day of working together, the chairman approached me. He said he reckoned I had saved him two years of work. He had an amazing insight into the new team that he would be working with and that was worth its weight in gold. The crazy thing is that this could have happened at their very first meeting, rather than during this consultant-led programme. When I asked them if they would have done it back at the coalface, they said 'no'; and when I asked them why not, they couldn't answer. They hadn't, until that moment, realised how important it was.

Outstanding leaders will understand this level of importance because they know how vital it is to get behind the mask that each person invariably wears. If you are always dealing with the image, then there are always going to be things that leap up and punch you on the nose. If you truly know and understand how each person in your team, and ideally your company, thinks and feels, many wonderful things can happen. The whole environment of trust can flourish because no one needs to hide anything. They can come and talk to you about any opportunities and concerns in the simplest and easiest way possible; you will be able to have discussions based on fact rather than perceptions; and all of this leads to improvement in business performance – and ultimately happier and more motivated people.

When I run programmes for teams that have been together for a while and I ask them to introduce themselves you can see their eyebrows go up in exasperation. 'Why ever is this woman asking us to do this? We've been working together for years for goodness sake, we already know each other.' The truth is that I've run over 200 programmes and found the responses are invariably similar. After we've been around the group and given a little of ourselves, people say things that include; 'I had no idea about what you had just shared', 'my perception of you has changed considerably', 'I had no idea you felt that way', 'I had no idea that you had those problems at home', and so on. A new team is frequently formed from the old one and new working relationships are created. These relationships are more effective, more honest and more open and result in a highly energised and higher-performing team. All this comes about through getting to know the real person behind the mask.

■

Of all the properties which belong to honourable men not one is so highly prized as that of character.

Henry Clay

■

I got a far greater understanding of this from Kevin Cashman's excellent book *Leadership from the Inside Out*. He refers to the two different states as coming from 'Persona' or 'Character'.

■

Character is the essence, the being of the leader, which is deeper and broader than any action or achievement. It is the essential nature of the person. In his essay on character, Ralph Waldo Emmerson wrote, 'This is what we call character – a reserved force which acts directly as presence, and without means'.

The purpose of character is to transform and to open up possibilities and potentialities. Qualities of character include authenticity, purpose, openness, trust, congruence, compassion, and creating value. When we are In-Character, we transform circumstances and open up possibilities and potentialities.

Persona is the personality or 'mask' we wear to cope with our life experiences. Persona is built to 'protect us' from external stressors, as well as internal fears, limitations and inadequacies. Our external shell can be either rigid and thick, preventing new possibilities to enter or to arise, or it can be permeable, thin and flexible, allowing learning and expression of potentialities.

The purpose of persona is to 'protect us' and help us cope. Qualities of the persona include image, safety, security, comfort, control, fear and winning at all costs. When we are In-Persona we seek to cope with circumstances. Even though many influences and circumstances are far beyond our control, we do control our choices. We are free to be whatever we want. We can be ourselves or not. We can be true to ourselves or not. We can wear one mask and another one later, and never, if we choose, appear in our true face. With these choices also come great costs. We may actually identify with the 'mask' as our true self. Then, later, we wonder at crucial moments why we lack effectiveness; or why truth evades us; or why life does not make sense; or why life lacks fulfilment or purpose. Our choice is free, but the consequences of not following the path to authenticity are great

Control versus openness: if our life energies are absorbed in control, we are In-Persona. This is particularly challenging if we are moving from managerial to leadership roles in an organisation. Managers control by virtue of their **doing.** *Leaders lead by virtue of their* **being.** *When we are (as often is the case) rapidly alternating between management and leadership, the relationship between control and openness is a constant dynamic.*

■

Whenever you meet someone new, just take the time to really get to know them. Ask them what they really feel good about in their life; what is their greatest challenge, what they would like to change in their organisation; about their children; about their hobbies; in fact, about anything that gives you an insight into who they really are, not just what they do. If you don't go to this level, I can tell you for certain that when you ask them about themselves they will only focus on what they do. You want to know what makes them tick, who they really are. The very best leaders care about 'the human being' not just the 'human doing'.

■

No man is free who is not a master of himself
Epictetus

■

ACCEPT RESPONSIBILITY 3

The greatest revolution of our generation is the discovery that human beings by changing the inner attitudes of their minds, can change the outer aspects of their lives.

William James

L eaders take 100% responsibility for every part of
their lives. How they think and feel, how they choose
to respond in each moment – and they don't blame
others for the circumstances of their being. This is the absolute key, and needs to be reinforced again and again and in
many different ways. It is the thread that holds everything
together and is largely misunderstood. Responsibility is
about owning every single thing that happens to you, learning to recognise that in each and every moment there is always a choice.

Imagine two CEOs in different organisations based in
Newcastle. They have just been told they are required to
do a presentation at a conference in London at 2pm that
afternoon. It is an important opportunity that cannot be
passed up, but it means changing their schedules and taking
a whole day to travel to London, deliver the presentation,
stay to network and then return. It is doubly inconvenient
as the end-of-year results are also due.

The first CEO thinks: 'What a great opportunity this is
going to be. I can travel in comfort on the train, and use the
time to get some serious thinking and planning done for the
meeting I have next week with the bank. The journey will
also give me the opportunity to prepare for the talk. I will
have the time to relax properly and maybe even read the
unopened book that's been sitting for ages on the bedside
table. I will be arriving in London at a time when plenty
of taxis are available for getting across the city. I always
enjoy taxi drivers as they have some fascinating stories to
tell. No doubt the presentation will be great because at the
last minute I noticed that a critical component was missing
and added it in. Hopefully, I'll get the chance to meet some

interesting new people before a comfortable journey back on the train where I can devour another chapter or two of the book. I'm looking forward to a really enjoyable and productive day!'

The second CEO thinks very differently about the day ahead: 'This is a real pain and not what the business requires at the present time. It means travelling down to London in the rush hour when the entire business world is also going. Trains are uncomfortable and draughty and there is no chance that I'll be able to concentrate on getting any work done, not least because of all those people with mobile phones stuck to their ears who find the need to talk twice as loudly as is necessary. So I shall end up worrying about the presentation all the way down and that will get me wound up. When I get there I will no doubt have to wait for a taxi, and the driver will then take me a long way round and charge me a fortune – these days you'd think you had put a deposit down to buy the cab! The presentation is bound to be a challenge. They are not really interested in what it is about, otherwise why would they invite me at the last minute? And, of course, the networking is invariably a waste of time, meeting lots of people that you will never see again. I am bound to be late leaving and then that long journey back. I'll be exhausted when I get home.'

These two CEOs now go to London to deliver this presentation. What sort of experience do they have? Pretty obvious really. One has a successful and enjoyable trip and returns home energised and happy. The other one has a mediocre experience and returns home irritable and tired. The reality of this situation is that the external circumstances are identical – same train, same taxis, and same people at the presentation, same networking opportunities. The only difference is the way they think. It's almost inevitable that their beliefs about the way things are going to pan out shape their respective days. Their thinking creates a day in their life. If it is possible to create one day, is it possible to create two? Or a week? Or a year? Or a lifetime? Are external circumstances responsible for shaping our lives or is it the way we think? I would like to suggest that it is the way we think, which is pretty exciting really as it means that in changing your thinking you can change your life. You have everything you need to create the life you truly want for yourself.

Outstanding leaders know this. They accept total responsibility for who they are and how they choose to respond in each and every moment – and they don't blame circumstances outside of themselves for any situation they are in. They know that between stimulus and response there is a gap, and in that gap is their moment of choice. Whatever we believe about a situation is how it becomes. You believe that today is a lousy day – that is how it will be. Taking total responsibility for your life is a daily challenge. Truly own your thoughts and your reactions. No one else but you is responsible for how you think or feel, for your happiness, your health, your work or home situation, your skills and abilities. Leaders do not believe they are a victim of circumstances because they totally own their responsibility. This is where leadership begins.

I find it tragic that so many people I meet in the workplace are not happy in their work and talk as though they have no choice but to remain there. Goodness knows what that is doing to their physical health as well as their state of mind. And when questioned about why they stay, it all comes down to security in some way shape or form, normally articulated as money. But where is security? If it is outside of you, where you have no control, you are always dependent on the outside world to behave the way you want it to behave. Well, that is ridiculous because you know that you cannot control the outside world. You may be able to influence it but control is simply not possible. Responsibility is saying 'I choose my life, I choose how I think and how I feel and in each and every moment I have that choice. I accept that my behaviour is the behaviour that I am choosing and I don't blame others for how I react.'

Until you do this in each and every moment you will not be able to change your circumstances or the situation that you are now in. Things will happen every day where you can choose to feel in command or out of control. Each moment is a life choosing moment if you can but be aware of it. There is no such thing as 'no choice'. Some choices may be more painful than others but they are still choices. If something ghastly happens to you, whether it's being made redundant or something much more serious such as an accident that paralyses you for life, you still have a choice. A choice about how you respond, how you choose to deal with it.

■

We who lived in the concentration camps can remember the men who walked through the huts comforting others, giving away their last piece of bread. They may have been few in number, but they offer sufficient proof that everything can be taken from a man but one thing: The last of his freedoms – to choose one's attitude in any given set of circumstances, to choose one's own way.

Viktor E. Frankl, *Man's Search for Meaning*

■

A company that made 3000 people redundant observed that there was a significant difference in the way individuals within the organisation responded to losing their jobs. All the people who had attended the programme focusing on responsibility chose to see what had happened as an opportunity and immediately put steps into action to create the circumstances that they really wanted. Virtually all the others went to the HR team asking for help and guidance. They felt very hard done by and wasted a lot of time moaning about what had happened. The circumstances were identical for both groups – nothing external to them was different. One group chose a very different response to the other group and, not surprisingly, got very different results. It enabled one group to free up their thinking and to come up with more possibilities and opportunities. Consequently, they had better outcomes. Needless to say, the people who thought otherwise and continued to blame the external circumstances for their difficulties didn't get the same opportunities.

Think of how you respond in the most ordinary circumstances. If you are driving home and the traffic is bad because of a really nasty accident on the motorway so the journey takes you twice as long, how do you behave when you walk in the front door to greet your family? Do you come in feeling happy and pleased to see them and greet them lovingly or do you walk in the door in a rotten temper, blaming the traffic and the stupid drivers who got in your way? If you do the latter – oh dear! The traffic is just traffic – that is not what has made you cross. It is the way that you have chosen to respond to it! You choose your thoughts, nobody else does. You can choose to sit in the car getting crosser and crosser, raising your blood pressure and your temper or you can make a different choice. You might sit there feeling very grateful that you are not the one in the accident, that you can relax and listen to some music or that book CD that you never seem to get time to listen to. You can think through and plan for that presentation you were going to do when you got home tonight so that you can have more quality time with your partner. If you choose, you can always find something valuable to think about or do. You could even appreciate the time to just 'be'. Getting home in a bad temper is your choice; it is not anything to do with the traffic. Once you truly accept this you then have other choices available to you because you are taking control. This understanding of choice is truly empowering. This is being a leader.

If you feel that someone else is pulling your strings, you are likely to be continually stressed and deliver to a less high standard than you are capable of. Leaders who live their lives in a constant state of stress make more mistakes, create unhappy relationships and can seriously demotivate their teams. They leave themselves open to illness as their body reacts negatively. If someone else is pulling your strings – in the case above it is the traffic – then you will feel permanently out of control. Not a great place for a leader to be. Great leaders do not blame the circumstances; great leaders take ownership of each thought, and each decision and every action they take. Ghandi is a fine example of this. He suffered continual violence and he chose peace at every turn. Whatever individuals or the government did to him, however awful or painful, his chosen response was to be peaceful. He knew that by making that as a conscious choice he would ultimately be the winner. Those who dealt with him were the ones who felt out of control because he did not respond in the way that they wanted him to – he refused to allow them to pull his strings.

What do you think Ghandi's beliefs might have been? How did they manifest in terms of his behaviour and how did those beliefs support him through some very tough years and some extremely challenging situations?

Think of the last time you 'lost it' in the office. What were the circumstances and who or what did you blame? How much were you demonstrating leadership behaviours? Now imagine that you had chosen a different response, one that you absolutely chose rather than reacting in the heat of the moment. How might the outcome have been different? How much more might you have achieved? Imagine after the bad traffic scenario, instead of walking in the door in a temper, you had walked in still calm and loving. How might your evening have gone better?

Now ask yourself: what are the beliefs that drive you and your behaviour?

- What do you believe about yourself?
- What do you believe about life in general?
- What do you believe about people at work?
- What do you believe about your team?
- What do you believe about management?
- What do you believe about leadership?

You may like to sit down and spend some time answering those questions and then reflecting on your responses. Your beliefs will drive your behaviours. How do those beliefs support what you want to become and what you want to achieve? Whatever you believe, that is how you will be and that is how you will lead.

Understanding responsibility at this level will change your life and blame will become a thing of the past. Remember, between stimulus and response there is a gap and in that gap is your moment of choice. Leaders become more and more aware of that gap and widen it when circumstances demand.

■

I would rather have a mind opened by wonder than one closed by belief.

Gerry Spence

■

LEADERSHIP IS ABOUT ME!

4

*Mastering others is strength.
Mastering yourself is true
power.*

Lao Tzu

We've looked at some of the qualities that make a great leader, but what is leadership really about? Fundamentally, it is about releasing human potential and possibilities. You need to be able to inspire your team, inspire them so they passionately want to become part of the action. You need to help them become focused and centred so that they are operating at their maximum capability. A critical component of inspiring others is that you must continually communicate to each individual your belief in them, their value to the group and the important contribution that they make. The confidence that you place in them contributes significantly to the confidence that they then have in themselves. This is where listening comes in as a critical skill. Listening to how another person thinks and feels, and giving them permission to express their innermost thoughts and feelings, brings to the surface the reality of the situation. This enables them to act.

So much of the time there is a belief that being a great leader is about changing other people. It isn't! To begin with, it is about changing and developing self. It is about changing the way *I* think, it is about changing *my* beliefs, it is about developing *my* abilities, and in so doing the world and people begin to change around me.

Great leadership involves putting responsibility where it belongs. It is neither about ducking responsibility and blaming all the circumstances around you, nor about taking the blame for everything and believing that all the things that go wrong have to come down to you. Instead, it is about recognising the reality of where you are right now, rather than the perception, and then continually moving forward to where you want to be. It is also the recognition that most of the time, when we put new systems in place to drive performance this is more about management than leadership.

Of course, we need to manage the business effectively, but principally the role of leader is to develop people so that they can perform at the very highest level.

Much research has been done into the nature of leadership and, if you have the time and energy to read it all, it will probably make good sense and will appeal on an intellectual level. However, will it inspire you to change behaviour? As the saying goes, doing what you have always done believing that you will get a different result is a definition of madness. If you read all these things and go on programmes that inspire you but you do nothing differently you are not developing your ability as a leader. Doesn't that seem like a waste of time and money?

The first key to great leadership, then, is to truly and at a fundamental level understand the meaning of responsibility. This is about recognising that in each and every moment we have a choice – there is no time when we don't have a choice. 'Rubbish!', I can hear some of you say. 'What about when a car knocks me down, when I'm made redundant, when my company decides to sell off part of the business?'

Let's look at one of these examples – you are made redundant. You have various choices about how you respond, e.g.:

- You go out and get roaring drunk.
- You tell all your colleagues how unfair it is and they are likely to be next.
- You phone your partner and tell them how truly ghastly this is and how you don't know how you are going to cope.
- You immediately pick up the phone to a head hunter and book an appointment.

- You tell your colleagues how you see this as a great opportunity to do something really different with your life, something you have always wanted to do.
- You invite everyone round for a party to celebrate your new life starting right now.
- ... and endless other possibilities.

It will be dependent on which of these choices you go with that will determine the outcome. Whatever choice you make, whatever meaning you give to the presenting circumstances will now impact what happens. You will begin to move towards the outcome from the very moment you decide how you are going to think about it. Your thinking will create your reality.

So much of the time it seems that the focus of leadership teaching is on how you get the best performance out of others and the skill sets you need to enable you to do that. My experience is that your impact will be far greater as a leader if you put your attention on developing *you*. Create a clear vision of how you want to be and then take 100% responsibility for living and working in each and every moment in line with that vision. If you want to look at an easy way to begin creating your vision go to Chapter 14, 'Where am I Heading?'. The knack of great leadership is to constantly recognise the gap between stimulus and response, and to keep widening that gap so that the choices become more and more conscious. Ask yourself how do you feel about your life – do you feel in control, in charge? Do you spend too long at work and blame the job for the hours you are working? Do you feel that you are pulling your strings or is someone else pulling them? Do you feel that you are making conscious choices or is the world a place where you muddle through as best as you can? Are you proactive or reactive? Do you say things like 'I am so disorganised, bad at time management, unfit, unhealthy, overworked?'. And at the same time do nothing about it as though some miracle is going to occur that will simply cause these things to change of their own accord?

So, focus your mind on becoming more and more aware of your choices and the responses that you make. How can your focus reflect the questions 'how can I develop me? How can I be more effective in every moment?'. The best leaders live their lives consciously and don't waste time on blaming – themselves or others. Their focus is continually on 'how can I change me to get a different result?'. In changing themselves the world responds by beginning to change around them. With less effort and less need to control.

On our Personal Leadership Programme there is a gap of at least two weeks between the sessions. When people come back on day three they talk about what has changed for them. The first question they answer is how they think they are different and typical responses include 'more tolerant, more open, receptive, appreciative, aware and authentic'. They then are asked what are they doing that is different and the responses include, 'truly listening, telling people how I value them, keeping my mouth shut and asking for their ideas, asking questions to get others to take responsibility'. The final stage is asking what results they are now getting. These include such things as 'improved motivation in my team, more openness from individuals, some brilliant ideas coming through, a real team now developing, higher quality decisions, improved relationships' and much, much more. I then ask them if they have been going round everywhere since leaving the programme and telling all their colleagues about it and asking others to change. Of course, they haven't. What they have done is focused on changing themselves and in doing so people and relationships have changed around them. This gives them the absolute proof that leadership starts from the inside out. It is not about changing others – it is about changing self.

■

Leadership is not so much about technique and methods as it is about opening the heart. Leadership is about inspiration – of oneself and of others. Great leadership is about human experiences, not processes. Leadership is not a formula or a program, it is a human activity that comes from the heart and considers the hearts of others.

It is an attitude, not a routine.

Lance Secretan, *Industry Week,*
10 December, 1998

■

COMMUNICATE RESPONSIBLY 5

It's very difficult to lead when people are not participating in the decision. You won't be able to attract and retain great people if they don't feel like they are part of the authorship of the strategy and of really critical issues. If you don't give people an opportunity to be engaged, they won't stay.

Howard Schultz

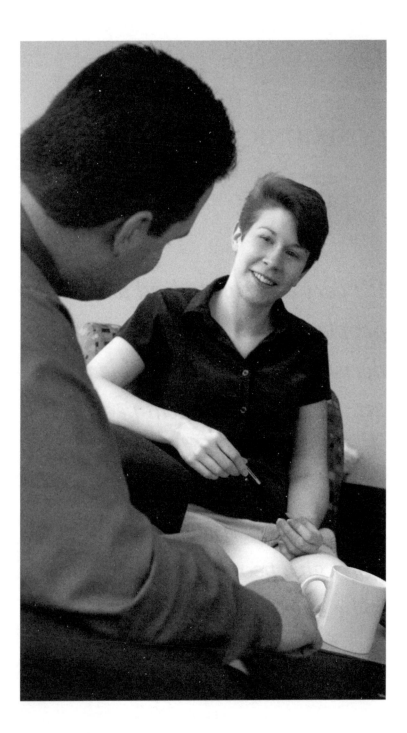

When you look at creating personal responsibility it is clear that it must go hand in hand with communication. How often do you tell people in your company what you want them to do and by so doing believe that you have handed them the responsibility to get on with it? You may be convinced of it and, at some level, they may believe it too. The reality is that you haven't given responsibility at all – you have told them what to do. If it doesn't work out, then in some way, shape or form, the blame will lie with you. To get people to take responsibility, they have to own it; they have to feel involved in developing the idea or the solution.

A retail organisation we worked with described the change of communication in this way. Part of the role of each one of the directors was to spend three days every week visiting the stores to see what was going on, to show real interest and, of course, to motivate the store managers to do even better. In retail, the majority of those who get to the top of the organisation have been in the sector for most of their life. They have come up through the ranks and know just about everything there is to know about running a successful store. So what are they looking for when they walk round the store? They are looking for things that are not being done as well as they could be! A typical approach in this organisation was for the director to greet the store manager at the door and walk around with him or her. The director would point out all the things that were going wrong and tell the manager how to sort it out. For example, if on their wanderings the director saw rubbish on the floor, or observed that some of the fruit and vegetables were wilted and it was only 10am in the morning, they would say: 'I am disappointed to see rubbish on the floor; this is not something that I usually see here. Can you make sure that everyone in the store is more aware of how the store looks? Fruit and veg looks a complete disaster and it's not good enough at all, particularly as we advertise this as our forte. Be sure to give the person in charge of this department some more training on how it should look – you need to get this sorted out immediately.' Or words to this effect. They would then go and have a cup of coffee together, and review the monthly figures to check on the manager's performance, and then the director would leave with a final word about sorting fruit and veg! From this interaction the director would mistakenly assume that the manager would be highly motivated to improve performance. The reality is that the manager is thinking that before the director comes next time he or she must be sure that there is no rubbish on the floor and that fruit and veg is sorted.

What is actually happening here is that responsibility is misplaced because of the way the director is communicating. The director is taking ownership of the problem and the solution when it should be the role of the store manager. After the directors understood the impact of this behaviour, their way of communicating became significantly different. Now, when faced with a similar situation, they do not offer advice and do not even comment on the poor areas they see, they just make a mental note of them. Over coffee the director asks the manager how things are going, and when the manager explains that there is a problem with fruit and veg, asks for the details. When he is told that the delivery lorry is consistently arriving in the middle of the day instead of 6am, the director asks several questions about how the manager is dealing with it and finally asks what support the manager would like. The manager now comes up with the solution, including asking for the support that he or she may require. Similarly, if the manager doesn't comment on the rubbish, the director may then point it out, but will immediately ask why the manager thinks it is happening. The director asks how the manager could deal with the situation differently so it doesn't happen in the future. The difference here is that the manager has now had responsibility firmly passed down to him or her and the director hasn't taken it on instead.

A totally different outcome is achieved. All because of a different communicating style. Instead of coming in and telling people what to do, using phrases such as 'What I suggest is; What I want you to do is; What I expect you to sort out now is', the director is asking probing questions, such as 'What do *you* think is the problem; how can *you* deal with it, what do *you* need to put in place; what support do *you* need from me?'

However, recognise that the first method described is much easier in the short term because, lets face it, you know all the answers. You have been there, done it, got the tee shirt. And, most of all, you care. You really want to help your managers be the best they can be, so you tell them how to improve. You want them to have the benefit of your wisdom, you want them to become outstanding, and so you continually tell them the best way to do it. That is not leadership. That is just proving how clever you are. This isn't developing other leaders. If you want people to take responsibility then you have to ask questions and then ask more and yet more. Telling them what to do not only discourages them from taking responsibility, it doesn't allow them to develop and, worst of all, every time they have another problem, guess what? They come to you!

Well, it is virtually impossible to become a great listener if you don't ask questions and merely spend your time giving advice. However, recognise that it will always be a temptation to give advice rather than ask questions because, in the short term, it is quicker. In my company's training programmes, when we demonstrate how to help someone think something through for themselves, the observation is always the same. Our trainees clearly see that giving advice is at best useless, and at worst dangerous. And yet if I ask them if they would like to give advice the response is invariably similar – most of them would! Even when it is a topic that they don't know much about! I don't think we ever lose the urge to share our ideas because, of course, we all want to be helpful. It is not part of our nature to become totally detached. In the organisations we work with, it is often the people from human resources who struggle the most. Their role, after all, is to help solve problems. They spend their time telling people how to do things differently. Meanwhile, line managers become accustomed to thinking that HR are there to sort out their problems for them. This is not a good idea as line managers can then step away from their responsibility while the HR department grows like Topsy!

Outstanding leaders require a commitment to communicating that is second to none. They see it not just as something that is interesting to learn and observe, but also as fundamentally important. They will develop this ability in every way they can, whether it is through training or the use of actors to give them immediate and powerful feedback. They will study the best and learn from them. And, most importantly, they will develop the ability to ask questions – and listen, and listen, and listen some more.

■

I start with the premise that the function of leadership is to produce more leaders, not more followers.

Ralph Nader

■

GETTING EVERYONE INVOLVED

If you want to build a ship, don't herd people together to collect wood and don't assign them tasks and work, but rather teach them to long for the endless immensity of the sea.

Antoine de Saint-Exupéry

I have discussed at various stages in this book the importance of communication and its strong links to responsibility. If we accept that the mark of outstanding leadership is not just how good a leader you are but the number of leaders you develop, then one of the key challenges is how you support people to think and contribute at the highest possible level in any group discussion, in order to achieve the most effective business decisions.

As leaders, we should not look at meetings as an opportunity to showcase our own talents and superior knowledge, although this is often what happens. Instead, meetings should focus on creating an environment that allows the whole team to contribute and work together towards generating the best possible outcome. One which they are all committed to achieving. A simple rule of thumb is to ensure that you focus more on the word 'you' than the word 'I' when it comes to thoughts and ideas.

Most meetings tend to follow a particular pattern. Those with the loudest voices and the most confidence are the ones who do nearly all the talking, half the time not listening to each other. There will often be confusion after the meeting as to exactly what actions have been agreed and there will be some people who rarely or never contribute at all. Does this sound at all familiar?

Let's take the last point first. Just because people are quiet, is it reasonable to assume that they do not have good ideas? I would suggest not. In fact, they often have some of the very best because they have been doing most of the listening and will have pulled together many of the most salient points from the various options proposed. However, if people are naturally quiet or perhaps a little lacking in confidence, they may need some encouragement to speak out in front of the group. As leaders, it is our job to ensure that everyone has a chance to contribute and, if necessary, to support them in the process. It is therefore important to ask those who have not spoken what they think, what ideas they have, how they feel the issues should be tackled etc. But, if you sense that they will be nervous, choose your words carefully when you ask for their input. For example, 'Bob, last week when we were talking about this, you had a couple of really good ideas, so please would you share your thoughts with the group?'. The fact that you have expressed your belief that their ideas are good will help them to develop the confidence to speak and once they have done so a few times, they may begin to volunteer their thoughts without prompting.

When it comes to hearing someone out rather than cutting them off in their prime, it can be a little challenging. We do this in various ways, the two favourites being simply interrupting someone, and by finishing their sentences for them (as if we know better than them what it was they were going to say). Either way, we have now taken over the air space to go on and express our own thoughts or ideas. There is a very interesting exercise that I include in my programmes which highlights just how much we cut into what others are saying. Most people are shocked to see just how much they do it and often argue that in a 'real situation' they would not behave in this way. My experience is actually quite the opposite. When they are back in the workplace, where they care passionately about what happens, they are in fact even worse! So, as leaders, we need to ensure that we allow people to express their thoughts fully, without interruption by us or those around them.

One of the things that I have found absolutely fascinating about this exercise over the years is that when it comes to measuring the less useful communication behaviours, some of the worst offenders are those who subsequently become trainers. As I said, when we are passionate about making a difference, we often become a little over enthusiastic in our communication. The people who are interested in working with us are always individuals who care tremendously about what they do, so I suppose it is inevitable that they tend to jump in with advice and ideas. However, it always comes as a huge shock to them.

Another way of getting everyone to listen to each other, rather than constantly interrupting and forcing their own ideas forward, is to let your team know that everyone who wants to will have the opportunity to speak on the subject for a limited time. Then you can allocate a time slot and go round everyone in turn. It might be 30 seconds, 2 minutes or longer, depending on the amount of time you have set aside for the meeting. If people know that they will get their turn to speak, then they are usually more prepared to wait and listen.

However, occasionally, there may be instances when time constraints genuinely mean that we need to move a discussion on. If this is the case, then applying the labelling technique (i.e. doing something and explaining why we are doing it) is acceptable. For example, 'John, thank you for sharing this. However, as time is moving on and we still have a number of items to cover, please could I ask you to make a note of this to raise at the next meeting, or put your thoughts in writing for us all.'

Of course, just listening does not guarantee that we will all understand exactly what someone else means. Remember, words often mean different things to different people and everyone may well have different types and levels of experience in the industry etc. Imagine a time when you have been in a heated discussion with somebody, only to realise some way down the road that you have actually misunderstood what they were trying to say. We all give meanings to words based on our own experiences. For example, when I hear the word 'powerful' it conjures up a sense of someone being really positive and vibrant, whilst for a colleague it may create more of a feeling of someone domineering and negative. So, we need to check out our understanding by asking questions and clarifying that we are all creating the same picture in our minds. As leaders we can help to generate this kind of interaction in meetings by regularly checking our own understanding of what is said, so that everyone can recognise its value.

If we can get everyone listening to and really understanding each other we have a great foundation upon which to build. From this we can create a sense of working together on the ideas. Often in meetings someone makes a suggestion or expresses a thought and around the room you can see people nodding and processing the information, then they will burst forth with an idea of their own. There is no acknowledgement at all that what led them to think this way was the previous suggestion from a colleague. Rather than teamwork, this creates a feeling of isolated thinking and a sense for the initial contributor that their ideas are no good. I encourage people to verbalise the process fully. For example, 'Joan, that's a great idea and we could also …', or 'Philip, thanks for making that suggestion because it got me thinking – how about if we …?'

In the first example, we have both supported the original idea and then built on it, creating a powerful sense of working together. The second example shows how we can still maintain this principle of working together, even when we don't necessarily agree with the original input – the important thing here is that we have acknowledged the value of the original idea. So, instead of feeling disappointed and marginalised, the participant will feel that their idea is a valuable part of the process and they are far more likely to continue to contribute.

In fact, this last point is a critical one. Creating an innovative and participative environment is not just about 'being nice to each other' and agreeing with everything and everyone. In fact, disagreement is vital to generating outstanding ideas, but we need to be sure of exactly what it is we are disagreeing with, which is why it is so important to really listen and understand the point that has been made. As leaders we need to ensure that our team listen with care and keep their disagreements focused on the subject, so that disagreement does not escalate into personal attacks, which are not at all helpful. This can happen if individuals feel that they are being ignored or are having difficulty expressing their point. It is our role as leaders to support them, by ensuring they have the opportunity to speak and by helping them to make their point as constructively as possible.

Outstanding leaders are not only brilliant communicators themselves, but they help to develop the communication skills of their people to create outstanding teamwork and the most profitable outcomes.

There is one final idea that I would like to share with you, which can help create outstanding thinking and contributions in any group discussion. If we want people to think at their very best, so that the ideas and proposals developed are of the highest quality, then we need to begin meetings on a positive note. Times may be challenging and there may be difficult issues to address, but then there is all the more reason to strive to lift spirits and open up minds. So start by going round the group and asking everyone to give an example of something positive that has happened for them in the past few days – you can choose whether you limit it to business. The energy in the room will lift and this will open the doors for people to think just a little better.

7

LEADERS LISTEN

*It is the province of knowledge
to speak and it is the privilege
of wisdom to listen.*

Oliver Wendell Holmes

The art of listening is crucial for leaders – yet it is a skill that is often overlooked. Listening should be developed to the point where it becomes second nature.

In my experience, senior people in business often feel that their prime role is to come up with ideas, and to make sure that they are able to sort out the business problems people bring to them. This is not the case. The role of a leader is to encourage others to think for themselves, to help them to feel that they own the problem, as well as the solution. Without this ability how can leaders develop people to take over their role when they move on?

I spend a lot of time observing and shadowing executives. Often, others see them as the main decision makers and, because that role is forced on to them, that is what they become. Universally we are prone to believe that people in positions of authority hold the answers. This belief is almost forced upon the executive and is reinforced by them becoming the one who provides all the answers. It becomes a self-fulfilling prophecy – a downward spiral in which executives have less and less time available for doing the things that they need to be doing, namely business development. Frequently, they are pulled back into daily maintenance activities. This results in them becoming increasingly stressed – and the whole life balance goes awry.

Yes, it may be quicker to give someone an answer when you have what you consider is the best idea to 'sort out the problem' and, in the short term, it's probably easier. However, what are the long-term benefits? In effect, you have said to the person 'you are not up to doing this without me'. You have also conditioned them into coming to you the next time there is a problem. A real lose/lose situation. Who has now taken responsibility for sorting it out? You have! And who is to blame when it doesn't work? For example, imagine someone coming to you asking how they should deal with the problem that the organisation is just about to lose a really big client. This is primarily the role of the sales team, but it could have a fairly nasty impact on the bottom line if it goes pear shaped. As you used to be the sales director before you became CEO, this is a situation you are all too familiar with. You feel you have some great ideas on how to resolve the problem. The temptation is to give advice and recommend your ideas on the solution. The minute you do this, certain things become clear. You are sending various messages that might include:

- They may not be able to do it for themselves.
- They cannot do it without you.
- You are likely to have better ideas than them.
- They have created the problem, but you can solve it.
- You will take responsibility for sorting it.

Certainly, this may not be the message that you think you are sending, but ask yourself, how do you feel when you tell someone that you have a problem and they immediately tell you how to solve it? Inspired? Put down? Encouraged? Insulted? Great leaders do not do this – they ask the appropriate questions and then they listen and listen some more.

Test the listening skills in your organisation or team by attending a meeting with the specific intention of observing, rather than contributing. On a piece of paper make a three column list. In the first column write the names of all the participants at the meeting. In the second column put the word 'interruptions' in the heading and in the third column the words 'question/listen'. Now, every time someone interrupts put a mark against their name in the second column. Every time someone asks a question of another person and listens to the answer put a mark against their name in the third column. At the end of the meeting, see where the balance of the conversation is. If there are lots of interruptions and few questions, then you have to ask yourself where the focus is. Is there genuine interest in other people's ideas, or is the predominant behaviour to get one's own point of view across? If you are in any doubt as to the consequences of not listening, read the article 'Rocket Science is not the Hard Part' in Chapter 1, 'Integral Performance'.

To truly listen, you need to engage your whole heart and mind, not just your ears. Words alone are an inadequate way of communicating. They mean different things to different people. If I asked everyone reading this book to write down the meaning of a word such as 'integrity' or 'empathy' you would be likely to write down some similar and some hugely different definitions. The point is that if your are in conversation with someone who has a totally different understanding of a particular word, there is a strong possibility that you will be talking at cross purposes and you will continue to hear the word with the meaning that you give to it. An interesting conversation ensues! Unless you are listening with every part of your being, you will not hear what the person is really saying to you.

Frequently, when someone wants to say something that they are nervous about saying, they will talk around the subject until they feel comfortable before getting on to what they really want to say. If you are not aware that this is going on you may miss a real opportunity because you are so busy thinking about what you are going to say next, or considering whether what they are suggesting fits in with your ideas, or you are busy looking for the areas that you don't agree with so you can tell them that they are wrong. The crucial thing here is the ability to let go of what is in your head and focus entirely on helping them to express what is in theirs. It is only when you fully understand what is going on for them that you will be able to deal with the *real* issues, not just the stated ones. In short, you will become a great leader by developing great listening skills.

One of the key findings of the 2006 'Best Companies to Work For' survey published in the *Sunday Times* is that leadership is vital for the top companies and, within that, listening is by far and away the most important factor.

The survey reveals that respondents working for the best-performing companies are enjoying a new level of engagement. Good employers value feedback and consult with staff much more than in previous years. Increasingly, firms recognise that engaging with staff improves their ability to recruit and retain quality people.

Recently, one of my clients who was part of the executive team said how she had always considered herself to be a good listener until she began to practice it in the way I am suggesting here. She said that it was in a conversation with the CEO that she changed her tactic completely. She proceeded to handle it without any feeling of needing to come up with ideas or respond in any way, other than support him thinking for himself. She said that she felt quite different – un-pressured and calm – that she listened and heard things very differently and, most importantly, she felt he came up with a far better and well thought-through solution. She felt that he owned the outcome more than if it had been her suggestion and, consequently, was more motivated to make it succeed.

Imagine for one moment a yellow brick road. A long, winding one that slopes gently down hill. At the bottom, there is a beautiful castle sparkling in the sunlight. The castle is not totally visible, as some of it is hidden by mist, but what you see makes you want to explore it. There are many roads leading off the road before you, and there are many people walking in different directions. Knowing where you want to go, you begin to walk down the road.

Coming towards you is a large group of people. You assume, as they draw level with you, that they will pass either side of you, but they don't. They behave as though you are invisible. They shove you out of the way, knocking you down and then trampling on you as they go past leaving you battered and bruised. Eventually, you pick yourself up, gather your thoughts and look around, trying to remember where it was you wanted to go. You start walking again.

This time, as you are walking, you see two friends. They are about to walk down one of the side roads and they call you over. They tell you where they are going and invite you to join them. When you explain to them that you are heading in a different direction they do their best to persuade you to go with them first, as you can go where you want to go afterwards. You like them, they are your friends, so eventually you agree and go with them. It is a pleasant experience and you enjoy it, but you know that it is not really where you want to go. You thank them and say goodbye and find your way back to the yellow brick road and, once again, start walking.

Suddenly you meet someone who blocks your path. They know exactly where you are going and they don't want you to go there. As you try to get past them, they become really aggressive and tell you that they will not allow it. They physically manhandle you away from the route you are taking and drag you off down a path that they want you to go down. At this point you give up. You let go of your wish to explore that beautiful castle and reluctantly follow where they wish to take you. After all, they are more powerful than you. Now, if there had been some policemen standing around watching this whole scenario it is possible that some of these people may have been arrested for physical violence against you.

I would like you to picture another scene. Imagine that you are observing a meeting of your peers. In this meeting there is clearly someone who has a great idea that they really want to share. However, every time they open their mouth, there are others talking at the same time, or interrupting them because they want to share their thoughts and ideas as well. Or, it could be that they seem to hear the idea, but they want to explore a different one first before they give another any serious consideration. It may be that the most senior person in the room is driving their own ideas forward because their opinion about the outcome is already formed. If you were to observe this meeting can you honestly say that this is something that never happens in your organisation? Can you truly say that this is something *you* never do?

What is the difference between this scenario and the one involving the castle? There is no difference – one is an example of physical violence and the other is mental violence. And every time you stop another person communicating this is, in effect, mental violence.

As a leader you want to have everybody in your team and in your organisation performing at his or her optimum level. For this to happen, it is critical for each and every person to feel listened to; to know that their ideas are heard; to know that they are going to be encouraged to think at the highest level they are capable of; to know that their creativity is being allowed to develop so their ideas are continually improving. Listening to another person at this profound level demonstrates to them that you expect great things from them and, by your listening, you inspire your people to reach for the heights of which they are capable.

We have been looking at leadership in the workplace but there are other places where the principles of good leadership apply. Step out of the business scenario for a moment, and imagine yourself somewhere else – at home for instance. Let's assume that you have children. If you are anything like me when I had young children, you love them so much you continually want to sort out their problems for them. I forgot that my role was really to encourage them to come up with the ideas for themselves. So, I spent much of the time not listening to them and, instead, telling them how to deal with their difficulties. It is easy now for me to see that it would have been more useful to have listened to them – to have offered them the space to work out the solutions for themselves. It was the same with friends who used to come to me with their problems. I busily suggested to them what they could do to sort themselves out, but I was blind to the fact that my suggestions were based on my own experiences of life, not theirs. My role was to listen, without interruption, and let them find the solution for themselves. The brain that has the problem nearly always has the solution – our role is to help the brain find new pathways, by listening and then listening some more. In every part of our life.

QUESTIONS, QUESTIONS AND MORE QUESTIONS!

You can tell whether a man is clever by his answers.

You can tell whether a man is wise by his questions.

Naquib Mahfouz

Outstanding leaders recognise that asking the right questions is critical for many reasons, not least because you must make sure you have all the relevant information for a situation before making a decision. So, becoming a listening leader is crucial. But it's not much use if what you are hearing bears little or no relevance to the situation that you are in.

So, why is it that listening and asking questions appear to be skills that are so patently undeveloped? Well, as we've already observed, we more often than not feel we can help and influence others by sharing our ideas, and giving them the benefit of our wisdom. Beneath this, we are perhaps hoping that we will influence them to think differently – to think as we do. The reality is that we rarely influence people to change their thinking by telling them our ideas. The human brain simply doesn't work in this way.

Imagine this: you take a pile of sand and pour a jug of water onto it. Some will soak in; the rest will flow down towards the edges, making pathways as it goes. Take a second jug of water and pour it onto the sand. Some may soak in and some will go down towards the edges, making new pathways. Most of the water, however, will flow down the existing pathways, making them deeper. This pattern will continue until, after just a few jugs, it will be virtually impossible for the water to do anything other than go down the established pathways.

The brain works like this. You have an opportunity or a problem and you begin to think it through. Pathways or traces are formed through the brain. Someone now tells you that you are wrong and you need to think it through again. The second time it is possible that you may find a new pathway. However, if someone asks you to think it through a third time it will be almost impossible for the brain to do anything other than go down the existing pathways.

As a leader you will find that using a conversational style – the 'no, try again' way – is really unhelpful. You are just making the thought become more entrenched. The only really effective way that you can have a positive influence in this situation is by asking questions – taking your people to different starting points and diverting their thought processes from their existing paths – and then truly listening to their answers. If you question your people and give them permission to search for the solutions themselves, – and you respect their efforts with careful listening – then you can stimulate powerful shifts in thinking.

Another point to bear in mind is that different types of questions will produce different types of answer. There are two types of question that are most commonly used – open and closed. There is another type which, in my experience, is significantly more powerful, and the most liberating – which I will discuss a little later in this chapter. First of all though, what is the difference between open and closed questions?

Open questions start with words like 'why', 'how', 'who', 'what', 'where', 'when'. These questions are looking for information and examples would be: 'Why do you think that this is the best approach?', 'How are you going to open that meeting with the shareholders tomorrow?', 'Who are you taking with you when you attend that meeting in the City?', 'What are you hoping to get from your trip to visit our new distributor dealership?', 'Where can you get the information that you require before meeting those new clients?', 'When can I expect the information that I require to enable me to prepare Friday's presentation?'.

Closed questions are the ones that are looking for commitment and they can be answered with a 'yes', 'no', or single word/phrase type answer. Examples would be: 'Would you like the red car or the black one?', 'Are you going to get this report to me today or tomorrow?', 'Have you finished the notes on the presentation that you are delivering tomorrow?'

Practising open questions is really important for everyone, in all kinds of situations. When you use a closed question, it is driven by your idea. You are the one in control and, should you choose to do so, it is quite straightforward for you to manipulate the answers. You will get a very powerful idea of how this can happen if you sit in a courtroom and listen to a barrister firing closed questions at the person on the witness stand and backing them into a corner!

Open questions, on the other hand, are asking for the person to say exactly what they think and feel without your guidance. That is, assuming that you don't continually interrupt with the great idea that you have just had! This type of 'open' questioning frequently needs to be learned, as most people are more naturally drawn towards asking closed questions. Fortunately, as people seem to like sharing what they think and feel about most subjects, they will usually need little excuse to keep talking anyway!

So, let's look now at an even more powerful type of questioning – a type of questioning that great leaders use.

Everyone has beliefs or limiting assumptions about themselves, about the situations they are in, and about the world around them. These beliefs can have an impact on the subconscious mind. They can prevent us from thinking well, hold us back from making good, positive decisions or lead us into poor quality judgments. For example, if for most of your life people have told you that you are no good at figures then, guess what? You will avoid figures, you will be nervous around them, you will continually tell people that you are no good at them and, not unnaturally, you will very likely become poor with figures. If you are promoted and an important aspect of the job is to read and really understand balance sheets, then something has to change – your thinking maybe! To unlock this part of your brain requires a different type of key and you can usually find this key by the use of *incisive questions*.

Incisive questions are not just interesting to learn, they are fundamental to being an outstanding leader. An incisive question is one that moves us past the limiting assumptions – or beliefs – that block our minds from thinking clearly. They free the mind to think afresh, to think creatively and to open up to new possibilities. Incisive questions also move individuals towards a greater level of responsibility – they own the solution.

A CEO I was working with recently on a 'shadowing' day proved himself to be an outstandingly good listener. He was open with everyone and asked really good questions. However, there were countless opportunities missed where, instead of making suggestions, he could have come back with an incisive question. For example, in one meeting it became evident there was a lack of communication between some of the teams in the division. The CEO listened to what was being said and gave a reasonably common sense recommendation about how to sort out the issue. Unfortunately, however, this included him shouldering responsibility for taking some action himself. He suggested that it might be useful if all the team leaders got together to discuss the importance and benefits of communicating differently. He then added that he would set up a meeting to hear what they were going to do to enable the learning to be disseminated to all other parts of the company.

Think about the assumptions that were probably being made by this CEO:

- There is a communication breakdown.
- They aren't aware of the communication breakdown.
- It is an organisational problem.
- They need me to sort it out.

By packaging up the solution and presenting it to the teams, wrapped and ready to go, various things have happened, which will have a negative impact:

- They teams don't own the problem themselves let alone the solution.
- The CEO has taken responsibility rather than leaving it where it belongs – with them.
- The CEO has now educated them into coming to him next time they have a problem.
- If it doesn't work out it can't possibly be their fault.
- He takes on another task, which eats into the time he should be spending on true leadership.

- There is a cost of this to the organisation – in time and effort.

And all of this because he missed the opportunity to ask the right questions!

How much more useful if he had said: 'It appears to me that there is a communication breakdown happening here. If you knew that this is something that you could resolve between you how might you go about doing it? If you knew that there would be huge benefits from communicating more effectively what do you think those benefits might be and how might you now choose to work together? If you knew that there is one thing that you could do right now that could have an immediate and positive impact what might that be?'

These questions are about challenging people in a way that takes them down different pathways in their brain – different from the ones they have already been down. There is a positive supposition in the question that suggests that there is an answer and that it is within reach of those who are being questioned. When questions are posed in this way they stimulate the brain to search for new answers. What is more, when incisive questioning is used within the context of a group the whole group collaborates to find the answer!

These type of questions – incisive questions – are not just interesting to learn, they are a fundamental requirement of an outstanding leader.

What you are doing is freeing up people's capacity to think – enabling them to see other possibilities and potentialities, to see that there are other ways of doing things, new approaches. If a member of your team is low in confidence they won't think well and you'll find it hard to instil new thinking in them. However, if you ask them the incisive question 'If you had 50% more confidence what would you say right now?' you offer them the opportunity to think beyond the constrictions that are holding them back. They will be able to consider further questions – 'how would you approach that meeting? ... what is the first thing you would say to your new boss? ... how might you approach the shareholders meeting?' – from the liberating position of 'What if?'. You are giving them permission to imagine new possibilities, available options and different outcomes. You are now in a position to support them in taking one or more of these actions.

Trying to convince someone that they can communicate clearly and concisely is likely to have limited impact if inside they feel they come across as muddled and waffly! They don't believe you! Worse still, you may now achieve the exact opposite of what you hoped because they now have to live up to your expectations of them. Asking a question that allows them to think of possibilities 'as if it were true' frees the mind from panic and allows new outcomes to emerge.

'If you knew you could communicate concisely and with clarity ... how would you phrase it? ... what might you do to prepare? ... how might you hold on to the key messages?'

It is not that you are expecting them to believe that all of a sudden they can speak concisely and with clarity. It is that you are allowing them to imagine this as a possibility so that they can come up with some new and different options.

This can take them from a feeling of panic to a new place of potential courage.

You have now opened this person's mind to the exciting possibilities of 'What if? and you can support them in taking some of the small steps that allow them time to develop gradually and without pressure.

So, how can you develop this questioning ability? By getting a notebook and, before every session, writing in the notebook the questions that you think you may be able to ask. In the beginning it is a good idea to have them all start with 'If you knew that ...', as then you know it will be an incisive question. There are, however, many that don't start in this way and they can become part of your questioning repetoire once you are more familiar with the process. Examples of these are:

- If you were in my position what advice would you give?
- If you were my boss what would you say to me now?
- Imagine the most powerful leader you know – what would he or she suggest now?

And so on ... Now read these questions out loud. You are bringing all your senses into play. Do something similar when the meeting is finished. Sit somewhere quietly for a couple of minutes and ask yourself 'If I knew that I could have improved that meeting with even better questions what questions might I have asked?'. Write those down too and read them out loud also. If you do this for a month you will retrain your mind to ask questions in a different way and you will be amazed at the impact. All the evidence I have to date suggests that these questions need to be learned. They do not come naturally but every leader will benefit enormously from developing them.

People mistakenly assume that their thinking is done by their head; it is actually done by the heart, which first dictates the conclusion, then commands the head to provide the reasoning that will defend it.

Anthony de Mello

I talked in Chapter 8 about the power of questions, and in particular incisive questions, for overcoming the limiting assumptions that hold us back. A limiting assumption is the perception that we have of reality, either about ourselves, a situation we are in or the world at large. So how do you know what question to ask? You can identify the assumptions that are going on in a person's head simply by asking them – 'What are you assuming that is stopping you …?'

Put the book down for a moment and think about a really big challenge that you are facing in your business at the moment. Now ask yourself the question, 'What am I assuming about this situation?'. Let's take an example that is real for me at this precise moment. I have a really tight deadline for getting this book finished at the same time as running a business. What might I be assuming about this situation?

- I don't have the time.
- The business will suffer while I am taking time off.
- Clients will resent it if I say that I am not available for a month – they may go elsewhere.
- Why am I bothering? The book may not sell anyway.
- I don't know if I can do this, I may not be good enough.
- My MD and team of directors are going to resent my taking the time to do this and won't feel supported.
- There is a huge cost to the business.
- It is the wrong time to do this.
- … and so on … and so on!

Now I ask myself, 'How well am I going to think through the actual writing of my book? … what will be going on in my mind every time I sit down to write? … what will be the quality of the output?' I would probably answer, 'this is not going to work!' All of this is mostly going on at a sub-conscious level but it certainly impacts every single decision that I now make. Each one of those assumptions could be turned around by at least one incisive question which could free my thinking.

- If you knew you could make the time, how would you now approach the deadline?
- If you knew that time is under your control, what are the things that you now need to let go of? How might you approach that?
- If you knew that the business will benefit hugely in the long term, how could you get the support you need to keep the business running smoothly in the short term?
- If you knew that you could take time out to write the book and keep the business running smoothly, what would you need to do differently – starting right now?
- If you knew that your clients will be perfectly OK and very understanding about this month when you are writing, how might you now tell them?
- If you knew that the book could become a best-seller if you position it in the right way, how would you feel about writing it?
- If you knew that you are good enough and you are capable of whatever you set your mind to, how would choose to express yourself?
- … and so on.

Please note – many of those assumptions might have a de-gree of accuracy but the purpose of this is to free my think-ing so possibilities can emerge as to how I can get the job done in the most effective way possible – the bottom line is the book needs to be written!

Learning to listen out for limiting assumptions is more than useful – it enables you to make decisions based on fact. Whenever you hear someone make a statement ask yourself if it is fact or perception. Some of the most dangerous ones are when people make value statements about another individual. Say, for instance, that you are stepping into a new role as managing director and there is going to be an overlap, deliberately, between you and the person who is departing. That person is now going to share with you all the perceptions that they have of all the people in your team. They will share these as though they are facts not perceptions. 'That person is very powerful and will dominate meetings. That one is good but rather lazy. Not sure how bright this one is. This one is a workaholic', and so on. The real danger here is that you believe everything you have heard to be a truth and then you manage the individuals accordingly. This is not useful at all because these perceptions may not reflect who they truly are. You will need to take all those statements and ask yourself important questions such as, 'If I knew that this person was a real team player how would I get the best out of him?', 'If I knew this person was highly intelligent what sort of things could I involve her in?'

I have frequently come across individuals who seem to be remarkably competent and are yet not delivering what they seem to be capable of. A new boss comes in and suddenly their performance improves considerably. Their lack of performance appears to be exacerbated by how they are being led. What assumptions might their previous boss have been making about them? Of course, you do also need to acknowledge that they must take responsibility for allowing their boss to affect their performance.

One director who attended the Personal Leadership Programme found this idea of removing limiting assumptions a little absurd. His opinion was that the problem was still there and you could not walk away from that. I agreed and asked him what he was thinking about in particular. He said that he had three people on his team and he thought they were stupid! I asked him, 'If you knew that they are actually highly intelligent how might you lead them differently?'. His response was, 'Well, if I really knew that they were intelligent I would hand over more of the projects to them, I would not check up so often on what they did, I would pass over this assignment that I believe I have to do myself', and quite a lot more. I then asked him if he would commit to doing those things. The look of scepticism on his face was interesting but, after a short discussion, he agreed that he would try. I phoned him three weeks later and asked him how the three 'stupid' people were doing. He didn't answer for a moment and then told me that their performance had improved considerably. Their lack of performance was nothing to do with them. It was to do with his limiting assumptions; so all it then took was one question. Performance in the team improved as a direct result.

Find out what people are assuming and then ask the right questions. Even when a meeting becomes blocked you can ask, 'What might we be assuming here that is blocking our thinking?'. Responses may include, 'Whatever we suggest no one is going to listen', 'There is nothing new to try because we have done everything we can', 'We are going to lose the client anyway.' Hear what the assumption is then remove it with a question that turns it into the positive opposite. If you knew that this time the boss is really open to hearing something new, what might you suggest? Recognise that this is not to change the perception. It is to free the mind to think of other possibilities, a true skill of an outstanding leader.

A colleague ran an in-house programme for a group of senior managers in a particular division. One delegate talked about how she had been newly promoted into a senior role and was now responsible for the team she had previously been part of. She was very open in discussing how challenging the role was and how, although she knew she was capable of managing the team, her thoughts about what the team might think of her being promoted were almost sabotaging her success within the role. When she left the programme on day two she was inspired to try something different. She came back on day three visibly more relaxed and positive. So what had happened? When she got back to work she sat down with a colleague and worked through her assumptions around her promotion, they went something like this:

- My colleagues will resent me.
- They will think that they should have been promoted, not me.
- They will not want to work for me.
- We won't then meet the team targets and objectives.
- I will fail in senior management.
- The directors will regret promoting me.
- At worst I will lose my job or be demoted back into my previous role.

These were just some of the assumptions! With all of these thoughts swirling around in her head it's not surprising that she felt stymied. Working through the key assumptions she was able to formulate incisive questions to move past these barriers to her thinking.

- If I knew that my team were truly supportive of me in this role, how might I communicate with them?
- If I knew that our team could be outstanding by working together, how might I achieve that teamwork?
- If I knew that I had been promoted because I was the best person for the job, what would I now do?

Each time she had one of those irritating assumptions bite back she asked herself an incisive question to counter it. The two week gap between days two and three of the programme had been a real turning point for her in terms of her relationship with her team – they had an amazing planning meeting which had given them the impetus to move forward and each individual had fed back to her how motivated they felt. She had not necessarily got rid of these assumptions. What she had done was to free her mind to come up with some new possibilities and opportunities – and then acted upon them.

10

DEVELOPING THE RIGHT PEOPLE

The best executive is the one who has sense enough to pick good men to do what he wants done, and self-restraint to keep from meddling with them while they do it.

Theodore Roosevelt

Outstanding leaders will always go for the right people; they are not interested in second best. They believe that the right people are their only really valuable resource. If you believe it is your role to motivate the people in your organisation then you have the wrong people. If you need to continually put new systems in place to drive your people then, quite simply, you have the wrong people. The very best organisations are interested in developing the people who have not only the appropriate attributes and skills, but who have outstanding commitment and focus – people who are totally dedicated to realising the vision of the team and the organisation.

Would you prefer to employ someone who has all the skills that you need but the wrong attitude or someone who is lacking in the skills but has the right attitude? The best leaders know that they are looking for people who will develop into the future leaders of the organisation and they want people who are passionate about what they do and are therefore motivated to deliver results. My experience is that organisations that are inclined to take people they feel really fit this mould even if there isn't a role for them are totally confident that the role will emerge and they will only add value to their companies. And invariably they do.

Maybe it would be interesting to have a team composed of the 'right people' and then let them work out the appropriate roles for themselves. Too often I see situations where the perfect person for the role is not found, so a decision is made to take 'second best'. Then time and money has to be spent on their training and development to get them to the required level of competence. Obviously you are focusing on their weaknesses rather than their strengths. You may then end up with a more rounded person, but how happy and fulfilled are they? How much passion do they have for the job? And what has happened to their strengths – the areas where they are naturally talented? Ultimately, you are likely to end up with a version of mediocrity, and the sad thing is that probably, through little fault of their own, they are now failing to deliver to the standard required and end up either leaving or being fired. They are unlikely to be adding real value to your bottom line.

Imagine a child at school who is outstandingly talented at maths but weak at geography. The temptation is to spend considerable time developing the ability at geography to get a well rounded person and broaden the talent. But, unless you are really careful, you end up with mediocrity in both.

The most outstanding leaders turn this whole idea on its head. When they have found the right people, then they start to look at how best to cover all of the responsibilities that need to be addressed, using the skills available. How many times are people promoted into management positions because they are performing really well in their current role? Does that mean that they will be the best manager for a team?

I have lost count of the times when I have seen really successful sales people coerced into management roles when they don't want to be in management. They love what they do and they are outstandingly good at it – why would they want to move? They are led to believe that it is important for their career to move up the ladder, otherwise they may not be seen as committed or ambitious. These people are hugely talented at selling, they love it and have a natural ability to build relationships, negotiate and close a deal. They do not have a natural talent for managing a team and don't even like it. The tragedy of this is that it is a real lose/lose situation for both sides. The 'manager' doesn't enjoy it, doesn't do well and ultimately is probably fired or leaves. The company not only loses an outstandingly talented sales person and the sales they were bringing in, but they probably now have a demoralised team of sales people who will present a difficult challenge for any new manager appointed.

This could so easily be avoided. By communicating effectively with their people, outstanding leaders begin to understand their future potential. So, instead of moving individuals into positions based on their history, they look for how they can create a role that will fully develop and exploit their talents.

There was some research done by the Gallup Organisation that showed some interesting results. These are published in the book by Marcus Buckingham and Donald O. Clifton – *Now, Discover Your Strengths*. They asked the question, 'At work do you have the opportunity to do what you do best every day?'. This was asked of 198,000 employees working in 7,939 business units within 36 companies. They then compared the responses to the performance of the business units and discovered the following: when employees answered that they strongly agreed with the question, they were 50% more likely to work in business units with lower employee turnover, 38% more likely to work in more productive business units, and 44% more likely to work in business units with higher customer satisfaction scores. And, over time, the business units that increased the number of employees who strongly agreed saw comparable increases in productivity, customer loyalty and employee retention. The conclusion is pretty clear. Whichever way you cut the data, the organisation whose employees feel that their strengths are used everyday is more powerful and definitely more robust.

It is critical to get the right people into the right job, where they can feel committed, excited and passionate about what they are doing. Organisations need individuals who are totally aware of their strengths, who want to build upon them and who know how to compensate for their weaknesses. They benefit from people who continually focus on the value they can add to the business, their colleagues and the overall development of the business. It is highly likely that waiting for all the right people to be in place before you finally define the company vision could save you many years of grief.

■

I am looking for a lot of people who have an infinite capacity to not know what can't be done.

Henry Ford

■

I have seen amazing things happen when you allow people the opportunity to work in an environment where the focus is to use and develop their strengths, where they are consistently told how well they are doing in that particular area, which keeps encouraging them to develop that ability even more. In such an environment, because they are naturally good at something, they feel passionately about it – giving more time, more energy and more commitment – and they achieve a greater outcome. At the same time, the need to put in more systems and processes to drive them diminishes. People view the world through their own mental filters – beliefs in other words. So, if they believe they are good at something, they will see themselves in that way and will naturally find ways to become better.

Each and every one of us is different. We think differently, we act differently, we view the world differently because of the different experiences we have had in our lives. You hear diversity being discussed in every organisation now. If we didn't have diversity in our organisations, if we were all the same, what would happen to creativity and innovation?

It would come to a grinding halt, so we know how critical it is. And yet, when we meet someone who thinks differently from us, rather than saying, 'Oh this is great, I am going to learn something different here', we spend our entire time trying to convince them they are wrong and they need to think like we do! Finding each individual's strengths and natural talents, irrespective of their colour, creed, sexual orientation, qualifications or background, is the way to build any organisation, as it stimulates ideas and encourages new thinking.

Get the right people first and then focus on their talents and their attitude. Support them in every way to build on those strengths, put them in the right place in the company, value them, treat them as equals and you will not need to employ managers to motivate them. Just make sure you don't allow anyone to demotivate them!

11

FLIPPING THE PYRAMID
– RELEASING PEOPLE
POTENTIAL

*If your actions inspire others
to dream more, learn more, do
more and become more, you
are a leader.*

John Quincy Adams

So much of the time, the role of a leader is seen as getting the best out of people. I disagree. For me management and leadership are different. Management is about making sure that the systems and processes are in place to drive people to perform to the highest level they can. It is more about control. Leadership is about inspiring them to do it for themselves. It is about freedom.

Think for one moment about how you would like people to treat you. I imagine you would come up with words and phrases such as:

- fairly
- kindly
- with integrity
- with respect
- listen to me
- value me
- encourage me
- with empathy
- allow me to be who I am without trying to change me.

Of course, we would all like that; who wouldn't? However, ask yourself the question, 'Can I make people treat me in that way?'. The answer is an emphatic 'no'. You might be able to influence them, but you cannot *make* them.

Now, when you understand this, it becomes clear that the reality is you have no control over what you *get*. And yet we spend a vast amount of time focusing on exactly that. There is an expectation that people will treat you in a certain way – from family and friends to colleagues. If they don't treat you in that way you are likely to be offended. You may even do your best to make them treat you in the way you feel you deserve and if they do not respond accordingly you continue to be upset. Even more scary is that quite often we have internal expectations of how they need to behave towards us and we don't tell them. We expect them to know! And then we get upset when they don't live up to those expectations! Recognising that the cause of our upset is actually nothing to do with them – that it is our own expectations – is authentic leadership thinking, because it leads us straight back to where responsibility lies.

However, even if you don't have control over what you *get*, you do have total control over what you *give*. So, if you want people to treat you the way you want to be treated, recognise that you need to treat them fairly, kindly, with integrity and respect, to listen to them, value them and allow them to be who they are without trying to change them. It is only in this way that you can exert any influence over the way people treat you. We waste so much time demanding that people treat us in certain ways; trying to get them to treat us the way that we believe that we deserve, trying to get the best out of our people, our teams, our salespeople. Changing your thinking – in effect turning it on its head – frees you up because you begin to focus on what you can truly affect without the need to control. Say to yourself:

- 'If I knew that I could give really great things to this person, this team, to enable them to be the very best they can be, what would I give them today?'
- 'If I really knew I could enable my team to do their job even better, build better client relationships, create more business opportunities what would I give them right now?'

When we do this exercise with executives they find it liberating. Instead of thinking about what can be done to get their people to be motivated – which frequently means putting in another system to drive performance – they imagine all the things that they can give to them to enable them to motivate themselves. It frequently includes really simple things such as:

- giving them more opportunity to come up with their own decisions
- giving them time to explore their thinking, more information
- positive feedback
- the chance to express their views
- more honest information.

It also allows them to have the chance to succeed or fail; the chance to be the best they can be.

Leaders let go of the things that they cannot control and focus on the things that they can. Embracing this level of thinking can have a huge impact on many areas, one of the most critical being confidence. The easiest way to describe this is by relating a situation I had with one of my clients. I was taking him to the airport following a one-to-one mentoring session. On the way, he started talking about a critical presentation that he was doing that evening to an extremely large group of very influential and high powered individuals across a broad spread of industries. As he was talking, it became clear that he was extremely uncomfortable about it. I asked him how he was feeling and his response was 'extremely nervous'. I then asked him what he was nervous about. His response went along the lines of 'I am worried that I am going to get it wrong, the message will be unclear, they won't like it and so won't listen to me, I will dry up at the critical moment, my voice will sound nervous and shaky'. I then asked him if there was anything else. A whole load more came out along similar lines. I asked him several times if there was anything else before he eventually ran dry! I then asked him the following question: 'Why are you thinking about you?'. He looked at me almost speechless, thought about it for a considerable length of time and then quietly said, 'Thank you.' In that moment he realised that all he was thinking about was *get*. What would people think about him, was he doing an OK job, would they think it was a good speech? He had absolutely no control over what people thought of him. His reputation was not inside him so he had no control over it. So, what was the point in worrying about it? There was only one thing he could do. Keep asking himself the question:

- 'If I knew that I could give some of the people there tonight a really enjoyable half hour, how would I start?'
- 'If I knew I could give them some excellent insights into what we are about and what difference going this route could make, how would I phrase this in the best way possible?'

He focused totally on what he could *give* and he let go of *get*. He phoned me a couple of days later, and said that his nerves had almost left him in that moment in the car and he gave probably the best speech he had ever given. He also said that he designed the speech very differently as a result of thinking in that way. Later he told me that this experience had been a life changing moment for him and at every meeting, every presentation, he always concentrated on what he could give and then let go of the rest. He believed that his confidence changed in that moment and he became much more effective as a leader.

I do a lot of public speaking and my mantra before I go on stage is always:

- 'What can I give that may enable individuals to look at things from a different perspective?'
- 'What can I give to just one person out there that will be useful to them and help them positively change their life is some way, shape or form?'

A client I was coaching was due to change her job and join another company. I asked her to describe her perfect job. It included things such as:

- A boss who supports and encourages me.
- A boss who gives me clear objectives and then gives me the freedom to do it my way.
- Friendly, open and helpful colleagues.
- An environment where learning and growth is encouraged and supported.
- The opportunity for rapid promotion.
- To be valued.
- To have my ideas heard.

I then asked her how many of these she had control over – how much could she make happen? The answer is clearly none – it is all focusing on *get*. I then asked her what might she need to *give* in order to create this job of her dreams. The list that she came up with included:

- Demonstrate to my boss from day one that I will think ahead – really show my commitment to taking the pressure off her.
- Be friendly towards my colleagues and never gossip about them behind their backs.
- Show genuine interest in them and remember little things about them that show my interest.
- Be happy to share work when things are busy.
- Find out important things I could learn so I develop myself and don't just rely on the organisation.
- Be open with my boss and share my goals and ask her to give me feedback.
- Always look for stretch goals.
- Listen to other people and, when they do listen to me, tell them how much I appreciate it.
- Tell my boss the things about her that I value.

Six months after starting the job, guess what sort of job she had? The job of her dreams!

A young client that I had was an amazing sales person. During seven years in selling she was head-hunted into new companies three times. She never took longer than six months to become the top salesperson irrespective of the product. And I don't mean top by a little way – I mean top by almost double the performance of the number two person. How? She said that before every customer visit she only ever had one thought in her mind, 'What can I give …?':

- 'What can I give to this customer so they really want to work with us?'
- 'What can I give to this customer so they can have the best service they have ever experienced?'

She never had to give the discounts that other sales people did, she brought in distributors that people had been struggling to bring on board for years, the distributors asked her to train their own salespeople, and she won all the awards – until she was head-hunted into the next organisation.

Imagine the impact on an organisation if each person within it began to think in this way. The CEO asking the question:

- 'What can I give to the board of directors to enable them to become more effective in their roles?'

It might include such things as allowing them more space to think for themselves, sharing more of your wisdom, more challenges to their current thinking, more opportunities to understand your concerns by being even more open and honest, more support to manage their life away from work, more appreciation. Now, imagine this way of being all the way down to the person who is closest to the customer thinking the same way. For example, the person on the till is now thinking:

- 'What can I give to this customer to enable them to have an even more enjoyable experience in this shop?'

Well, I can give them:

- a smile
- my time
- my help
- my support
- a shop that looks even more welcoming
- and so on.

It is less about 'How can I get the customer to spend more money?' and more about 'What can I give to this customer so that they have such a great experience that they may want to come back again and perhaps spend a little more here than go somewhere else to spend it?'

It is truly about going against tradition and turning the organisation on its head – about placing yourself, as the most senior leader, in a foundation role so that you are providing the support to everyone in your team. What …

- information
- knowledge
- wisdom
- support
- listening
- openness
- appreciation

… can you give to each person you meet in your company each and every day to enable them to become more and more who they truly are? If each person at every level of your organisation thought and behaved in this way, you would have some very happy clients and a truly high performing organisation!

▪

> *A leader is best when people barely know he exists, not so good when people obey and acclaim him, worse when they despise him ... But of a good leader who talks little when his work is done, his aim fulfilled, they will say, 'We did it ourselves.'*
>
> **Lao Tzu**

▪

12
DEMONSTRATING VALUE

Argue for your limitations, and sure enough, they're yours.

Richard Bach (Illusions)

As leaders in your organisations, you know that your role is to raise performance at every level and with every individual. If you can just get the best out of the people you have employed, then you will get greater impact on the bottom line.

I want you to imagine that you have just had a great weekend away, everything is going well in your life and the business is doing okay. Could be better, but pretty okay. You wake up in the morning feeling full of energy, the sun is shining and you are looking forward to a great day ahead. What now happens during this day while you are feeling in this great and strong place? Everything that you touch goes well, doesn't it? Every conversation, every client visit, every meeting seems to go better than usual. And all because you are feeling good about yourself and the world.

This is so obvious that it hardly seems worth saying and yet, somehow, we don't translate that into how people are treated at work. When I ask the people I am training what feedback they get on their performance, the answer is usually along the lines of: 'Well, I get told when I am getting it wrong!' So the focus is on problems or weaknesses rather than strengths. And yet that doesn't make sense. If you want to improve performance, then you want people to feel good about themselves, to feel strong and able to keep developing. If you focus on people's strengths they develop and grow these strengths and their weaknesses become less relevant.

Think of a time when you were delivering a really high-powered presentation to some of the captains of industry or senior colleagues. When you came out several people approached you and said, 'That was outstanding, best speech I have heard you give. You took a very complex subject and made it come alive in a simple and understandable way. I have now got a real grip of the issues and challenges our industry is facing.' How do you feel and what do you want to do next time? Do it even better! And, because what was said to you was so specific – 'you took a complex subject and made it come alive in a simple and understandable way' – you now know what you can build on and it may be even better next time. Someone has focused on your strength and naturally you want to develop that strength even more.

We are all very good at focusing on what we are bad at and considerably less good at stating our strengths. An exercise I often do is to get two individuals working together and then ask one of them to share with the other person what they feel really good about in themselves. Shock, horror! I then ask them how easy it would be to talk for five minutes about where they are not so good. Easy, is the reply! Well, if we want to become the best that we can be, how useful is it that we find it easier to focus on our weaknesses, to carry a belief that we really are not good enough in so many areas? What we believe, we become. In many ways we can become our own worst enemies. What is more, we are also inclined to look for the same in others.

So, what typically happens in business? Leaders look only for the weaknesses that people are demonstrating and then they tell them how they can improve them. If that is where the focus is then the likelihood is that you will see more of their weaknesses because that is where the attention is. Instead of looking for what they are truly good at and supporting them in developing that area, the focus is all about what they are weaker at and getting them to pay attention to that.

Picture this. As an employee, you are doing a fairly basic and undemanding job where you have a lot of customer interaction such as working on the till at a large supermarket.

In this situation, your organisation is very committed to customer service so it is drummed into you at every available opportunity that this is critical. You are aware of this, especially as your manager keeps reminding you. However, on a daily and weekly basis, no one ever tells you what a good job you are doing. Nobody notices the little things you do such as smile at all the customers, help an elderly lady out to the car with her shopping, remember little things about your colleagues and show interest in them, search the store for a product that the customer can't find and generally go out of your way to do the best you can. No one appears to notice and certainly no one tells you. How might you go home feeling at the end of each day at work? How might you now treat your partner, your children, just because you don't feel valued? What might happen to your work output, your commitment to your job and your organisation?

Now, imagine the opposite possibility. You have a boss who notices every little thing that you do well and makes a real point of telling you. Each time he notices something what do you then want to do? Do it even better, of course! Improved customer service happens without any effort or need to be reminded. You feel valued and you go home at the end of every day feeling really good about yourself, your job and your environment. Because you feel good, you now behave differently towards those nearest to you – their day improves.

So why does the focus so often go the other way? My observation is that most of the time, it is for the best reasons – it is because we care. This is especially noticeable in close relationships and even more so with children. We love them so much that we don't want them to make the mistakes that we have made (and hopefully learned from) throughout our lives, so we keep telling them they mustn't do things in a certain way, they should do it in the way that we know is successful. We do it for the very best reasons a lot of the time but we then forget to notice and tell them all the wonderful things that they do, however little. How often do you tell them that their bedrooms are messy? How often do you tell them when it is a little bit tidy? I rest my case! Please don't hear in this that you must never criticise. There are occasions when it is appropriate – we just need to get the balance right.

■

The spirited horse, which will try to win the race of its own accord, will run even faster if encouraged.

Ovid

■

This applies at every level and, in my experience, it is even worse the higher up in an organisation you go. Very few directors tell each other when they see something that they have done well. The big things, yes, but these are less frequent of course. Also, people on executive boards often forget how lonely a CEO's position is. Many CEOs I work with say to me that they get all the bad news and lots of criticism. However, no one seems to notice let alone tell them that they have done a good job, handled a meeting well or dealt brilliantly with a difficult situation. And yet, they are expected to feel good and deliver outstandingly well all the time – after all the buck stops with them. How much better would they feel and then perform if someone just told them what they do well occasionally? I frequently get people who I work with complaining that their bosses never appreciate them and I then ask them how good their boss is. Normally they say something along the lines of pretty okay. My response is to ask them when they last appreciated their boss! Embarrassed silence!

There is constant research coming out from numerous sources to support this theory – the 2006 'Best Companies to Work For' survey published in the *Sunday Times* said that people feeling valued at work is what makes the difference to the work environment and consequently to performance. This is not really surprising and yet somehow when it comes to praising people the words stick in the gullet. There is this assumption that, because there is no criticism, people must assume that they are getting it right.

One managing director, who I worked with, began to recognise that maybe his behaviour had been adversely affecting one of his directors. He believed that this individual was underperforming and had possibly been over-promoted so he was therefore having real difficulty dealing with this person. He decided that he would begin to focus on the individual's strengths and stop telling the director what to do all the time. In as little as two weeks, the director's performance changed in a truly remarkable way. When I next saw the managing director, his words to me were, 'His lack of performance was nothing to do with him, it was to do with me.' This also demonstrates how a belief can drive behaviour. The MD had beliefs that this individual was not up to the job firmly set in his mind and was, therefore, managing him accordingly. Managing the person in this way was just reinforcing the behaviour of the individual and the circle was now complete. Breaking the circle, even though the MD admitted to having little confidence that it would achieve a positive outcome, caused the breakthrough. The MD was totally amazed at the dramatic and almost transformational reaction from his director.

Sadly, appreciating people is not a typical part of the British culture. It is not macho to keep telling people what they are doing well. And yet … I challenge you! For the next month make a point of telling every person that you come into contact with the things that you value about them; perhaps it's the service that they give you; whatever you notice that sets them apart in the way they behave, anything at all that you can see as a strength – tell them. Not just as a 'thank you', but really tell them as specifically as possible what it is that you value. If you do this, you could start a revolution, or perhaps an evolution. You will begin to see amazing things happen – I guarantee it! Relationships will improve, performance will improve, you will feel better in yourself and you will begin to achieve more. Aim to tell people what you value about them at least four times more than you criticise them. And, incidentally, don't just keep this for the workplace. You are a leader in every part of your life and that includes home. So often we take our partners, our children and even our friends for granted, and even if we appreciate them very much we don't tell them. Notice all the little things they do and tell them the value that they have for you – how very much you appreciate what they do for you, just for being the special person they are. And don't forget *you*! I am not suggesting that you rush around everywhere telling each person how wonderful you are. But, each evening before you go to sleep, think of at least one really good thing that you did today. Try it! See what happens.

■

Treat people as if they were what they ought to be, and you help them to become what they are capable of being.

Goethe

■

13

WHAT STYLE OF LEADERSHIP?

Pull the string, and it will follow wherever you wish. Push it, and it will go nowhere at all.

Dwight D. Eisenhower

There are discussions going on all the time about the different types of leadership. One week you will see in the paper how the best leaders, the ones who really get results, are those who come in with all guns blazing and turn around a situation really quickly – getting rid of the 'dead wood', restructuring, changing the systems and processes and so on. Others will say that, no, the best types of leaders are those who really care about people, who involve, support and encourage them.

Maybe there is a need for both – in one person. When we went to work with Bedfordshire Police the Chief Constable who had just taken over was Michael O'Byrne. At that time Bedfordshire Police was not doing too well in any of its performance measurements. It was one of the worst in the country. Michael knew what needed doing and, in his words, he became a dictator for the next two years. He then knew that he needed to do things differently. To date, he had been driving the change, and everyone had little choice but to join in. However, the changes were his ideas and driven by him and therefore nobody else really owned them. Now he needed to do things differently to make the changes sustainable. He recognised that he needed to change his style drastically. In his own words …

▪

When I became Chief Constable in Bedfordshire the force was one of the worst performing both locally and in the country, across a whole range of measurements, such as crime detection and response times. I had worked in the force before, so I knew we had good people, which made it hard to understand the poor results.

The first thing I addressed were the systems and procedures, putting in place appropriate checks and processes so that we could really pinpoint activity and outcome. This had a considerable impact and improved our overall perform-ance significantly. However, we then reached a plateau and it seemed impossible to move beyond this point.

I'd worked with Penny previously and decided to talk with her about the challenge I was facing. Her experience with other clients going through change processes was sim-ilar. Systems can only go so far, then it starts to become more about the attitudes and behaviours of the individu-als. I needed a catalyst to create a breakthrough and the Personal Leadership Programme (PLP) seemed to present the answer.

This was a very different type of intervention to any-thing we had used before, so I decided that I should expe-rience it first. That was all it took to convince me that it was exactly what we needed. Starting with my top team, we managed a roll-out throughout the force, by training up an internal team of trainers. It is difficult to describe the buzz that went through the whole organisation as a result. The positive impact on individuals was unlike anything I had witnessed in my thirty-odd years as a police officer.

So what was the bottom-line effect? This is always more difficult to show in a non-profit making public organisation as there is no profit and loss or share value indicator. What can be said, is that at the beginning of my tenure as chief, the force was one of the poorest performers in the country and the annual inspection by Her Majesty's Inspector of Con-stabulary produced a report highly critical of most of the key operational areas, making 19 recommendations for im-provement. At the end of five years it had become one of the best performers in the country across the whole spectrum of agreed performance measures and the annual inspection by the HMI resulted in only one recommendation. That was in an area where we had already recognised performance was poor and were already working to improve.

From a more personal perspective, I was able to retire knowing that the 'good work' would continue, because the results were not simply about me 'kicking ass', as is so often the case with a leadership role. Instead, we had created a situation where individuals were prepared to take on the responsibility for future performance and were ready to run with it.

■

What I am not suggesting here is that you are two different people. I know too many executives who have one style for home and another for work and occasionally the work style overlaps into inappropriate behaviour at home. I have a colleague who, before he left to run his own business, was an extremely successful senior executive in a global business. He travelled the world developing senior managers and directors in various countries and he helped mould people into the shape that the organisation required. He did it by telling them exactly what they needed to do and how they needed to change. He used every training programme and every method available, developing them to the companies' required level of excellence. He believed that he was a really good leader. Then one day, in conversation with his wife, he had a serious wake-up call. She announced that even though she loved him as her husband she hated him as a human being! This was a real defining moment. Until that point he had regarded himself as successful, but in what terms and against what criteria? Yes he was achieving the business objectives but if he were to change his behaviour and choose to be the kind of leader, the kind of human being that he really wanted to be, how much more successful might he and those around him become? He will say that at that moment his life changed. He now works with top teams developing them in a very different way with powerful results.

If you are the type of leader who can go in and make a big difference fast then good on you, if that is what is required. The challenge is this: people may see you making all the decisions, see you as the guru of the change, and become less and less likely to make any decisions for themselves – after all they might get it wrong. Plus, there is the added risk that because of the pressure you are putting everyone under they become stressed, fail to think well, make less effective decisions leading to more pressure and even poorer performance until they eventually leave. In a bad situation it is invariably the best people who leave first.

One of the pertinent examples of the risk around this style is Lee Iaccoca who became president of Chrysler in 1979. He totally changed the way the company operated. He made massive redundancies, completely redesigned the entire management structure, put in new systems, controls and processes in finance, quality control and production. He virtually browbeat the unions into accepting the changes that had to be made by threatening bankruptcy if they didn't go with him. He worked a miracle and the results were amazing – it was written about everywhere as one of the most amazing turnarounds. However, once he became distracted with other things and the focus of the turnaround became blurred things went pear shaped pretty fast. Some years later Chrysler ended up near bankruptcy. Because the change was driven totally by him, individuals at every level of the organisation were used to taking instruction – they didn't have to think for themselves. They hadn't learned how to take responsibility. So when they needed to, they didn't know how or were too frightened.

For me, the mark of outstanding leadership is twofold. It is not just about being a great leader yourself, it is about developing other leaders. Chrysler could be a perfect example of the one without the other. When he was actually in the driving seat and totally focused, things went really well. When he took his eye off the ball he hadn't developed any leaders to step into the role.

Conversely, the example earlier in this chapter shows that not only can we achieve even greater results when we are developing our people, but they are sustainable, even after the leader is gone.

Two very different styles can both be effective and used in different circumstances and at different times. So is there a 'right' and 'wrong'? I would suggest that there is only a choice and that choice comes back to 'Who do you want to be?'. There is clear evidence that there are occasions when bringing in the 'hit man' can have immediate and dramatic results. But are they sustainable? Interestingly, in the research done and written about in *Good to Great* by Jim Collins there were none of these high powered charismatic people at the top. The CEOs who were driving the change were not brought in from outside. They were individuals promoted from within, they did not have big egos, they had extreme personal humility, they were not interested in hierarchies – they believed in their people and supported them to become the best they can be.

There is a need for both styles. Imagine that you are a very senior police officer and a significant crisis occurs – you get called to a situation where a group of young people are being held as hostages in a school. The person holding them is armed and extremely dangerous and has already killed some of the other schoolchildren. In these circumstances you are certainly going to want a highly competent individual who is going to be decisive and able to issue commands in a clear and concise way and expect everyone to jump to fulfil those commands. When the immediate crisis is resolved you are going to need a very different style, one that is open and encouraging and where asking questions and listening are top of the agenda. How did we do? What can we learn from that? How could we improve it so we get the hostages out even quicker next time? The difficulty can be that if your natural style is to tell people what to do all the time, when you ask them their opinion they are unlikely to give it. It may not be safe. They may not be as good as you and could get it wrong. They may come up with an idea that you think is stupid. However, if typically you have the opposite style and only step into the telling style when time is short and the risk of rejection is low then you are much more likely to be able to take people with you.

Some senior people that I come across in organisations get confused and end up falling somewhere between the two styles. They really want to let go and give the decisions to the team but they come up with comments such as 'just fly it past me before you make any decision'! Then, of course, they put in their own ideas as well. On top of that they often won't quite make a decision either. People end up very confused and a leader like this can be one of the most difficult leaders to work for. Most often this can happen when you have someone who has been either the brains behind the company or has taken it to new levels during their tenure. They are then really nervous that someone may not do it as well as them or may not do it 'their way'. They know at a logical level they need to let go but at an emotional level they are still holding on. That is a serious failure, as people really aren't sure where they stand at all.

The choice is yours. The first step is to choose at a deep and fundamental level who you really want to be. Only then can you decide which style you want to develop. Understand and develop the behaviours that support that style – and then deliver – consistently.

■

The Way to do is to be.

Lao Tzu

■

14 WHERE AM I HEADING?

Reach high, for stars lie hidden in your soul.

Dream deep, for every dream precedes the goal.

Ralph Vaull Starr

One of the things that can be observed about really outstanding leaders is that they are very clear about who they are and where they are going. So many people live their lives taking each day as it comes but then complaining when things are going wrong. They focus all the time on what they don't want without any clear idea of what they do want. If you don't know what you truly want then any old pathway will do.

Think of an organisation that doesn't really know what products it wants to make, what market place it wants to be in, what sort of clients it wants. How successful will that organisation be? The obvious answer is 'not very'. It will spend its time trying different things, getting frustrated when it doesn't work out and then trying something else, with each new idea and initiative costing time and money. Individuals will become confused, standards are likely to be flexible to say the least, few people will be delivering to a high standard and priorities will change almost daily.

For an organisation to be really successful there needs to be total clarity about where it is going and the strategy it is going to use to get it there. If this is true of organisations why wouldn't it be the same for an individual? The truth is that it is the same but we just don't realise it. Sit down for an hour and really imagine that you are a plc. What would you want that plc to be doing, what would you want it to achieve if anything were possible and you simply could not fail? What might be the pinnacle of success for 'you plc'? What wonderful relationships would you have in 'you plc'? What would you be doing to be healthy and happy in 'you plc'? Let me say it again – if you don't know where you are going then any old pathway will do.

How much of your life do you put off until tomorrow? How many times do you think of the things that you would like to do, if you only had time? How often do you make commitments at the beginning of the New Year about all the things that you are going to do differently – stop smoking, lose weight, go to the gym? How many of them do you actually stick to? Why does this happen? I suggest that it is because the focus is in the wrong place and the attention is all on what do I need to DO differently, what behaviour I need to change. It is all about doing rather than being. Coming from the former it is easy to walk away and to say, well there was just wasn't enough time, it was too difficult because … Coming from the latter is a very different choice and is about making a choice at a heart level or at a values and character level.

Try this as an exercise. Write your obituary as though you have just died and your best friend is writing a eulogy about you and your life. Write it completely honestly and really think about what they might say about you if they were being completely honest and speaking from the heart. How would they remember you? Would they talk about what you did and what you achieved? What are the successes that would immediately spring to their minds? Would they talk about the funny things that you did and said? Would they talk about the value and joy you brought into their life? When I did this many years ago I then showed it to my best friend and was really pleased when she told me it was very accurate! There were many good things but clearly there were some not so good things which showed me in stark clarity the bits of my character that needed considerable attention.

When you have done this write another obituary as though you died at a really wonderful old age. In fact write several – one as though your best friend were writing, one as though one of your children were writing, one as though your partner were writing and one as though a work colleague were writing. How would you really like to be remembered? Really imagine what you would want them to say about you, how you would want them to think about you, what are the things about you that they would have really loved, how would they have felt that you had expressed the music in your soul, what are the things that made them proud and what made them love you. What is it about you that will leave a lasting memory of your uniqueness? Deeply imagine this and make it come as alive as possible. Now read it carefully and ask yourself, 'Is this primarily about what I do or is it about who I am?'. Does it include things such as '... was such a very loving person; ... was always there to support me even when I failed; ... gave of their time to really listen to me; ... made me feel special'? Now make the choice about who you really want to be at the most honest and profound level possible. Then and only then, compare the two obituaries – the one as if you died right now and the one where it is years later. What do you need to change so that you receive exactly the kind of obituary you have just written? Having made the true decision about who you want to be, now think about what the behaviours are that you need to change, what do you need to do differently. Outstanding leaders know who they are and that is what drives the behaviour. There is purpose behind everything and it resonates in all that they do and say.

Having identified how you choose to be you can now move on to what you want to do. You will already have got some clues from the first exercise but now it is worth spending a bit of time creating a vision for your life. An easy way to do this is to imagine the best six months of your life. Not a six months that you have already had or the following six months but a six months of your dreams! Imagine that you are enjoying your ninety-fifth birthday celebrations and you are standing up telling your nearest and dearest about this amazing six months that you had. Pretend that you have a magic wand and anything that you can imagine is possible. When you do this, it is important to allow yourself to consider all options without judgement – let go of thoughts such as, 'That is completely unrealistic – I couldn't possibly achieve that.' If you were describing the very best six months of your life, exactly as you would like them to be in your deepest dreams, how would they be? What would you be doing in the different areas of your life – your work, career, home, hobbies, relationship, family etc. Ask yourself the question, 'If I knew that anything and everything is possible, what would I be doing?'. It is important to be as clear as possible when you do this. If you are describing the sort of home you are living in, be specific. For example: 'My home is in the country, surrounded by beautiful views, a river at the bottom of the garden and lots of magnificent trees in the garden. The house has large rooms and is light and sunny. There is a huge family kitchen with an Aga to cook on. The whole house has a feeling of being welcoming and friendly and people love spending time in it. It has a library and a conservatory to sit in on the warmer evenings,' and so on. When you write this, describe everything in the present tense, as in the example above. If possible, do this on an extremely large sheet of paper so you are allowing yourself space to expand if you wish to add things later.

■

Make no little plans. They have no magic to stir men's blood and probably themselves will not be realized. Make big plans. Aim high in hope and work. Remembering that a noble, logical diagram once recorded will not die.

Niccolo Machiavelli

■

This may sound like a slightly fanciful exercise but it really can produce some fascinating results. It frees your mind to think of new possibilities and opportunities, it gives you something to aim for and it gives you the opportunity to face one thing: you can achieve whatever you want if you just focus and then do the little things each day that move you closer to where you want to be. Too many people, when asked what they really want in life, will start to tell you, after the first sentence, what they don't want. Day-to-day life takes over and they have no clear idea of their vision – until they retire! One individual that I worked with shared a personal trauma that was giving him some deeply personal challenges. His younger wife had run off with an older man and couldn't decide who she wanted to be with. When I asked this person what his vision was for his life he waffled! When I asked him what he thought his wife's vision was for her life he replied, 'She likes shopping!' When I asked what the vision he and his wife had for their life together was, he made it up in front of me. What chance would you give that relationship?

If you choose to do this exercise you may find that something strange will happen. Can you remember the first time that you bought a new make of motor car? When you took it out on the road for the very first time? I will bet that you thought that many other people strangely had the same idea on the same day – there suddenly seemed to be so many more of this make of car on the road than you had ever thought. The reality is they were always there, you just didn't notice them before. The only thing that has happened is that your focus has changed. If you draw your vision and just put it in a place where you can see it each day something strange seems to happen. Opportunities appear like magic. Of course, they were always there but you just didn't see them before. Create the vision, believe it with passion and you will find yourself moving towards it almost without doing anything else. Get some action behind it and you will be unstoppable.

Whereas I have described this as an individual exercise it works just as well with families, with teams and with boards of directors. I use it often and the new ideas that emerge and the energy for action that it creates never cease to amaze me. It is enjoyable, helps visioning come alive and it also includes values by default. You are not just talking about what you are going to do but how you are going to be, how you are going to feel, how other people are going to see you.

I did both of these exercises over ten years ago. They have helped me become the leader that I now am. They helped me identify my strengths as a person and they helped me identify the areas that needed considerable work. I still have those exercises from all that time ago and looking at them again I can see how far I have come. Without them, would I have come so far? Not a hope!

▪

Until one is committed there is hesitance, the chance to draw back, always ineffectiveness. Concerning all acts of initiative (and creation) there is one elementary truth, the ignorance of which

*kills countless ideas and splendid plans: the mo-
ment one definitely commits oneself, then Provi-
dence moves too. All sorts of things occur to help
one that would otherwise never have occurred. A
whole stream of events issues from the decision,
raising in one's favour all manner of unforeseen
incidents and meetings and material assistance,
which no man could have dreamed would come
his way.*

W.N. Murray,
The Scottish Himalayan Expedition

■

15

LIVING IN THE PRESENT

To think is easy. To act is hard. But the hardest thing in the world is to act in accordance with your thinking.

Goethe

So much of our time is spent in the wrong place – either agonising over a mistake we made yesterday or worrying about whether that new client is going to give us the business that we so urgently need.

Outstanding leaders don't do this. They recognise that the past cannot be changed so there is no point worrying about it. They will choose to look at it in a way that identifies what lessons might be learned from the experience. They may need to go and make reparation for something they have said or done. They will certainly make a note of the mistakes and how they can do things differently in the future. And then they move on and are unlikely to think about it again. They look reality fairly and squarely in the eye.

As to the future, they will most definitely spend time being clear about where they want to go in differing levels of detail. However, they clearly recognise that there is only one place where they can make the change – in the present moment – and that is where they focus their attention. Worrying about the future is truly futile. There are only two types of things that you can worry about – things you can control and things you can't. If you can control it then do something about it so you don't need to worry; if you can't do anything about it what is the point of worrying?

Now link this type of thinking to beliefs which I talked about earlier. The story of the two CEOs who had to go to London for the day to do a presentation clearly highlighted how our thinking creates our reality. So, if we continually worry about something that might happen in the future and that is where our thinking is then, guess what? We begin to draw those very circumstances towards us.

Every moment of your life, there is only one place where you can make a difference, only one place where you can make changes, only one place where you can influence others, only one place where you can improve relationships, improve team performance, improve your own abilities as a leader – in the present moment.

I have listened to Roger Black, the Olympian, speak on many occasions and have heard him talk about the Olympic race in which he won his silver medal and how he prepared for it. He will talk about how he had a life changing moment when he realised that his challenge was to run his perfect race. Not worry about the people he was competing against, not worry about the training that they were doing and whether it was going to give them a better edge, not worry about anything other than running his own perfect race. He describes the feeling of running that race, how he felt and how he thought. His entire focus and energy was in each and every step he ran, he didn't think about what was happening outside of him. All his focus was on him running his best race ever. He ran outstandingly well and won an Olympic silver medal – he will say that for him this is his gold medal because he knows that he ran his perfect race. A little known fact is that Roger actually beat his personal best time. He let go of everything outside of himself and focused on what he could give in the present moment. His performance demonstrated that focus. That is where transformation can happen and only there.

To get a high performing organisation there are many things that need to combine and a truly important part of this is being sure that every single person has taken ownership of the company vision and the strategy and then be passionate about it. However, passion alone will not get you there. Passion needs action behind it and that can only happen in the moment. How many people do you know who leave a conference, training programme or inspirational speech truly energised and determined to do things differently? What all too frequently happens? That inspiration leads nowhere because life takes over and it is far too easy to slip back into the 'usual' way of doing things. They forget that the only way things are going to change is if they take action – in the present moment.

■

Truly understanding the concept of living in the present quite literally transformed my life. Not on the outside – to all intense and purposes I still do many of the same things and have many of the same relationships, but the way in which I feel inside in each and every moment about all of these things is totally different.

Think about the times when you have a really intense experience, one that is life changing and one that you will never forget. It may be witnessing the birth of your child, it may be attending an incredibly special performance by an outstanding artiste or perhaps reading a book that has a profound message for you. In these cases, what happens is that we become totally involved and 'lost in the experience' and this creates a clarity which touches all of our senses and makes it unforgettable. Close your eyes now and remember one of your life changing moments and you will know what I mean.

Now, instead of this being an occasional experience for me, it happens every day. Not that I have reached a Zen state by any means, but I have many experiences every day that I am consciously there in the moment with. It has helped me to appreciate the world and the people around me to a much greater degree. I am no longer constantly worrying about what might happen next or dwelling on past troubles. The effect is that my life is less stressed, happier and certainly more fulfilled, which means that I am able to give more to those around me.

Director, Merlin Marketing & Mentoring Limited

▪

As a leader this is part of your role. Wherever you go in the organisation you need to be sure that you are asking the right questions that support this philosophy. Far too often when I am shadowing a director in an organisation I hear questions being asked that have absolutely no relevance to the strategy or the vision. They are probably low level questions that indirectly tell the person that it is the less important day-to-day activities that you care about far more than the real guts of the business. Asking a question that makes it clear what your passion is and linking it to what they are focusing their attention on in the present moment is what sends the message loud and clear.

For example – let's say that an important component of your vision is to become the number one company in 'Best Companies to Work For' because you are clear that happy and motivated people give better results and improved customer relationships. What are the sort of questions that you might ask on your 'walk around'. Maybe something along the lines of:

- What have you been doing this week to enable your team to feel more empowered?
- How many of your team have come up with new ideas to improve performance this week?
- How much of your meeting this afternoon will be focusing on improving relationships, internal and external?

- What are you and your team doing differently each day as a result of the commitment to becoming number one in 'Best Companies to Work For'?

A lot of the time people are unhappy in their jobs because they are worrying about the future – will they get that promotion, will they land that new deal, will they get a good appraisal, will that presentation be OK and so on. Rather than focusing on the present they choose to be worried and unhappy because of something that may happen in the future. What a waste of energy and how stultifying for good performance! If they could just bring their energy and focus back to the present moment they may find they could actually enjoy what they are doing right now and, consequently, become more effective at doing it. Keep asking people: 'What can you do now, in this present moment, to affect …?'. The more you can get people to focus on what they can do now – in the present moment – to effect an outcome, the more they will respond. They will find that they can achieve more, have more control than they realised, and begin to take greater responsibility.

■

In order to be utterly happy, the only thing necessary is to refrain from comparing this moment with other moments in the past, which I often did not fully enjoy because I was comparing them with other moments of the future.

André Gide

■

16

COMPANY CULTURE

The great leaders are like the best conductors – they reach beyond the notes to reach the magic in the players.

Blaine Lee

What is company culture and where does it start? It starts from the top and is the cumulative effect of all the processes, systems, information, relationships, behaviours and attitudes of each person in the organisation. It is the sum of everything we have looked at in this book. The foundation blocks are the behaviours of the leaders within the organisation. In my experience, all too often when people come in to leadership roles within companies, at any level, they immediately rush into 'doing' – doing something, anything that will get quick results. They feel that they need to make their mark in some way. Their team has probably been waiting for the new boss to arrive, with a certain amount of fear and trepidation, or maybe even hope, dependent upon their experience of their previous leader. Just suppose that instead of rushing into 'doing' you spent a considerable amount of time really getting to know the people you are going to be working with. Not just finding out about their surface image, but finding out who they are at a human being level – discovering what lies behind the mask.

The person at the top will dictate the style. If you have a CEO who is ex-army, very dictatorial and very good at decision making then rapidly the behaviours will change to accommodate that. Or, of course, some of the people who are not happy with that style will leave, possibly to be replaced with individuals who the new CEO has worked with before. Others in the top team are likely to become pussy cats round the boss, accepting that this is now how it has to be. They refer final decisions and become uncomfortable challenging those of the boss. The interesting outcome now is that, although they become like that with the new boss, inadvertently they adopt some of this dictatorial style when managing downwards. Bit by bit the culture permeates all the way down. What also happens is that more and more systems and procedures end up being put in place to measure performance and drive everyone to conform. Responsibility at individual level diminishes as more and more decisions get passed further back up the line. Decisions slow down, people become demotivated and the best people leave. Bureaucracy rules!

However, it is amazing how quickly one can begin to change these circumstances when a different type of leader comes in. Someone in a senior learning and development role, lets call him Simon, who I worked with recently told me how six months ago he was looking for another job and was on the point of leaving his organisation. And then the new director arrived to become his boss. He described this man as the embodiment of everything that I talk about in this book. The impact this man has already had has been amazing. I know the company will become infinitely more successful and will become an employer of choice. Simon is now totally passionate about his job, lives and breathes the values they espouse and is raring to go to embrace and be a significant part of the changes that are coming. He is excited to be part of the team and the organisation. All this in six months.

So to develop the culture that you want, firstly have the courage to truly choose it. Then everything needs to be aligned. It is no good saying you want an organisation that is open and listens if the current communicating style is all about 'I'. It is not going to help if you tell people they are empowered, but then keep changing the priorities or getting in the way of the decisions they have just made. It won't work if you have a value statement that says 'we trust our people' and then you put in systems and processes that check and monitor every single thing they do. It will be impossible for people to really understand responsibility if you say you want them to take it and then keep telling them what to do. It is no good saying you want a company that believes in equality if you then create a structure with many, many levels in the hierarchy and where you so obviously have very different levels of perks for the people at the top.

■

Inequality still runs rampant in most business corporations. I'm referring now to hierarchical inequality which legitimises and institutionalises the principles of 'We' versus 'They' ... The people at the top of the corporate hierarchy grant themselves privilege after privilege, flaunt those privileges before the men and women who do the real work, then wonder why employees are unmoved by management's invocations to cut costs and boost profitability ... When I think of the millions of dollars spent by people at the top of the management hierarchy on efforts to motivate people who are continually put down by that hierarchy, I can only shake my head in wonder.

Ken Iverson, from his 1998 book *Plain Talk*

■

I have people who I work with who keep telling me things like 'my organisation is so political', 'my company has a dreadful blame culture', 'the real culture here is one of fear'. Well, an organisation cannot be political, only people can play politics. Blame can only happen if individuals are consistently looking to blame someone for the mistakes that are made. Fear cannot exist unless individuals are being threatened by other individuals. It is nothing to do with the 'organisation'. The culture is developed by the behaviour of each individual. So own it, take responsibility for the fact that you are part of that pattern and commit to changing your behaviour. I mentioned in Chapter 1 the company where everyone was espousing the idea of the 'political organisation' – we were doing a roll-out of the programme and every single group within the organisation that attended came up with the fact that a major part of the problem in the organisation was that it was so political. I asked which of them were playing politics. They looked shocked and said that of course it wasn't them! We then asked every single group we met and their response was identical. Who was fooling who? Even using the language 'we have a political organisation' allows a ducking of responsibility and a good excuse to do nothing to rectify it.

Imagine for one moment that you choose to be the sort of leader that we have been espousing in this book and you are taking the role of CEO. You, with your top team, create a truly inspirational vision that you are 100% committed to. You demonstrate this by every action you take, by every question you ask and by the way you talk about it with passion. This you do consistently. Now imagine that each person you employ is the right person primarily because of their attitude – they can buy into the vision and have the strengths to support the direction in which you are taking the business. You empower them to deliver because you don't need systems and processes to drive them, they are self motivated and self disciplined to deliver everything that is required. They want to be part of a winning team so they recognise that they must fulfil their role by giving their very best. Communication lines are open in all directions, so everyone is comfortable with passing back up the line the consequences of the decisions that don't work out. They all listen at every level and continually focus on each other's strengths. Each person values their colleagues and tells them so. Differences are acknowledged and valued. At every level in the company each person is seen as a leader. They are each focused on *give* not *get*, all the way through to the customer.

Now imagine that this is happening in your organisation. What would be the impact? And not just on you and your employees, but stretching far beyond. If every one of your employees goes home at the end of each day feeling valued and knowing that their contribution is helping achieve the vision, how will they treat their partners, their children, their friends? How will they feel, what choices will they be making in each moment because they feel worthwhile? How will their beliefs have changed because of these incredibly improved circumstances? And because beliefs drive behaviour how might the behaviours change?

So what can you do if you are not the CEO? How can you change the culture then? That may not be as easy but it is still possible to make a significant impact. Having chosen what sort of leader you wish to be, at whatever level you are at, then take 100% responsibility for that choice. Live and breathe all the values and behaviours that support it. Work with your team in those ways so they become committed to a similar way of working. Support a culture to develop in your team, your division and then allow it to expand outwards. You can become the culture in which you intend to live your life and, in so doing, you may just inspire others to become great leaders as well.

Blue sky? Let me assure you it is not! I've seen people change their lives in two weeks by thinking and behaving as true 'leaders'. I've witnessed how many lives they have affected directly and indirectly. To me, this is what true leadership is all about. To have the courage to truly choose who you want to be and then live it and breathe it in each and every moment. To do the small things such as listening, questioning and showing appreciation. To take responsibility for your thoughts, actions, reactions, failures and successes. To create leaders out of every person you meet.

Leadership … challenging? … difficult? … stressful? Absolutely … but only if you choose to believe so.

∎

People are always blaming their circumstances for what they are. I don't believe in circumstances. The people who get on in this world are the people who get up and look for the circumstances they want, and, if they can't find them, make them.

George Bernard Shaw

▓

THE PROOF OF THE PUDDING

A change of approach pays dividends

When Penny called to ask me to write a piece for her new book it caused me to ponder, not for the first time, how best to calculate a true bottom-line value for the training programme we call PLP.

The intangible benefits are impressive. We have been able to establish a common language and a common set of skills to underpin our core values. More than that, we have a body of well researched evidence that affirms why they are critical to the long term-health and success of the business.

Employees at every level in Lucite International became aware of the destructive power of the 'shut out'. Managers throughout the organisation willed themselves to believe that 'the brain that had the problem also had the solution' and forced themselves to combat years of conditioning and not leap in and solve their subordinates' issues on the first occasion that they paused for breath.

Senior executives became used to starting meetings with an invitation to describe something positive that had happened to them in the last few days, either from a business or a personal perspective. Many asked if they could offer both a personal and a business example. Gradually recognition dawned that this simple technique was helping them to maintain a balanced perspective, even when discussing potential problems. It didn't make the problems less significant but it did enable them to be addressed in a more positive fashion.

Many employees found the techniques had wide ranging applications in their personal lives as well, particularly those with spouses, partners and teenage children. In fact there are many great examples of individual impacts that have arisen as a result of people attending the PLP workshops, whether in building or strengthening relationships, or achieving goals which they had thought would take them many years. They have had, in some cases, dramatic effects, but it is still hard to calculate a bottom-line effect. Then I remembered another example – one which was close to home and which had arisen as part of my preparation to become a PLP trainer.

Four years ago I was working hard to master the PLP material and to learn to apply some of the techniques. One area that concerned me more than most at the time was my ability to facilitate a thinking session. This is where you support someone to think for themselves, particularly with the use of incisive questioning. I knew I had to practise. I phoned one of my team and asked her if she would mind being a 'guinea pig' while I fine-tuned my technique. She was happy to be helpful but a bit concerned about what we might talk about. My attention was focused on the process rather than the content so as long as we found something to talk about I was not overly worried.

We met a few days later and she decided to share her worries and frustrations about the way in which employee relations on her site were progressing. Gradually, as is often the case when someone is worried about something, a somewhat negative picture emerged. We were moving from an environment where all our wage negotiations had been conducted centrally to one where they were being carried out locally. As a result the local employee representatives were required to take real responsibility for their actions for the first time.

It wasn't really anyone's fault but she just didn't think that some of the main players on the union side were going to be able to support changes even if they agreed with them. I had wrestled with the same problem myself over the years and I felt inclined to agree but I resisted that temptation and recalled another of the phrases from the PLP – 'What you focus on gets bigger and stronger, what you ignore withers and dies.' From somewhere in my head the following question emerged: 'These guys are good at so many things; if you were looking for positives what would they be?'

She paused for a moment and looked at me as though I hadn't been paying attention. Then she forced herself to address the question and, gradually at first, she produced a stream of positive descriptions. 'They have good values … They share the same goal that we do of providing a long-term future for this site … They're always very courteous in their approach and dealings with me.'

Suddenly the same people who a minute ago had been the obstacles to progress began to sound like potential supporters of change. More importantly she felt differently about them. She began to see that with work, support and belief there might be a way forward.

As we moved further into the session, my confidence grew. I asked her what steps she would take to make progress if she knew that the employee representatives had the same goals that she had. Now that she was free of the shackles of the limiting assumption that her employee representatives had a different agenda to her, she generated a whole series of creative initiatives to pursue.

One that sticks in my mind was to ask a local contact that she had if she could bring a group of employee representatives and managers to his site to meet their managers and reps and to understand how they had developed a working 'partnership'. Three months later that meeting took place. It was a real catalyst in helping to move our employee relations at this particular site from the traditional conflict model to the much more participative and constructive model of partnership.

Such changes do not come easily and both managers and union representatives can find it more comfortable and feel less exposed in the traditional approach but, four years on, relationships and trust are much stronger. The business has benefited because local negotiations have been conducted and results achieved that contribute to the shared goal of long-term job security at the site. At the end of last year two of the most senior reps (with minimal input from the management team) communicated the details of a new working practices agreement that they had negotiated with their colleagues. That deal, along with many of the others concluded in the last three years, has contributed to a significant improvement in the success of that particular site.

I'm not suggesting that the facilitated thinking session I conducted was solely responsible for the change but the shift in attitude and the belief that things could be different sprang from that session. It was the catalyst. The thinking changed and the results followed.

Four years on, I'm more confident than ever of the powerful impact of the programme on our people and our business.

Kevin Leith
Personnel Director
Lucite International

Major financial institution

I have never been convinced that stand-alone skills training is the answer to developing people and, when it comes to leadership, I have always believed that it was more about communicating and inspiring people. Back in 1998, my search for a development programme for our leaders within the insurance division of one of the major banks provided me with some interesting and, in some cases, downright weird options. It wasn't until I met Penny for a coffee at Waterloo Station that I suddenly became confident that I had found what we needed.

Having sent a couple of colleagues to test out the Personal Leadership Programme, I was amazed at the impact on them, so I decided to experience it for myself. I had been looking for something different and that is exactly what I got. It was difficult to understand as it was not that the content was exactly new, but the way in which it was linked together and the common sense approach suddenly gave me some startling and, quite frankly, challenging insights. In particular, the concentration on who we want to be as leaders and the importance of responsibility really resonated.

We started to roll the programme throughout the division. The results we experienced were astounding, not least because we were not making any startlingly major changes, just what appeared to be small and straightforward ones. For a start, meetings were transformed into really productive experiences, with those attending totally motivated to act, just because they had become more aware of their communicating styles. Leaders were brimming with enthusiasm about the programme and I was spending much of my time listening to and coaching managers who were now overflowing with ideas on how they wanted to be and what they wanted to do differently.

When my boss moved to a significantly larger division of the bank, he felt that the PLP was the way forward to create the cultural changes necessary to transform the business. I trained as a trainer of the programme and we took it throughout the organisation over a two year period. The result was that we developed a more responsible, empowered and enlightened workforce and this was really highlighted when overall changes to our structure demanded some widespread redundancies over our division and others. Of course, this news was hardly warmly received in any area, but the contrast in attitudes between individuals in our division and in others was remarkable. Instead of downing tools, seeking counselling and generally behaving as victims, which was the typical reaction, our people remained dedicated to performing at their highest level. The majority of those who were eventually made redundant took it as the first positive step to a new and different future.

There is no doubt in my mind now that my initial instincts around stand-alone skills not being enough were valid. Through concentrating on how we were being and our attitudes, what we managed to create was an extraordinary level of personal responsibility, which not only benefited our organisation, but also had a truly transformational effect on the professional and personal lives of our people.

Kirsten Campbell
Director
Quintessential Limited

Leadership is all about cherry pies

Would you imagine that something as simple as a freshly baked cherry pie could make a substantial difference to a business?

Well, here's the proof.

In the summer of 2003, one of the largest food retailers, started to move from a period of recovery towards a period of growth. Things were looking more positive for the business, following a very difficult trading period after the purchase of a rival chain. For the first time in many years, the organisation felt ready to seek the views of employees and listen to them.

This is how the former Head of Organisational Development, Sally Pattison, tells the story:

> *The staff feedback survey indicated that there were many good things happening in the business, for example people were generally happy with the pay and the benefits that they received. However, as anticipated, it also indicated that the organisation had an issue with employee engagement.*
>
> *We were very keen to fix this problem, as our research had shown us that improved employee engagement led to improved customer satisfaction and who wouldn't want that? Improved customer satisfaction is quite a big prize for a food retailer as improved customer satisfaction obviously leads to improved sales. Sales are one of the key measures that the city use to judge the performance of the organisation. This in turn would lead to an improved share price, organisational growth and sustainability. We started to look for a solution that would address the needs that we had. We needed to focus upon:*

- *communication skills*
- *meeting behaviours*
- *listening skills*
- *responsibility*
- *motivation.*

We knew that if we were going to change the way people behaved in the business, we needed to get them to look at who they truly were. This wasn't about management skills or behavioural training, this was about personal leadership at the deepest level. Not long after, in July 2003, we started to work with Penny and her team and agreed that 2000 managers across all of the stores and all of the business support functions would attend the Personal Leadership Programme.

The programme launched and it wasn't long before we started to create a hunger for people to attend the programme in the business (we even had a waiting list of attendees). The managers loved it, and soon began to see how making small changes in their thinking and their behaviour could make a difference to the results that they personally achieved in the business. The managers were keen to tell us what was going well and what they had achieved and we were keen to listen. We wanted to tell the business about the difference our managers were making and to celebrate our achievements (even this was a significant change of behaviour for the business). More importantly we wanted to create a hunger and energy for change within the business. We knew that we had to change the way we behaved if we wanted to change the results that we were getting and we, like most organisations, wanted better results.

I want to share with you the first good news story that we ever received from one of our store managers; it's an important story because it is the story that shaped the way we talked about good news and the results that the programme was getting across the business.

Every week, in all of our stores, the store manager holds a meeting with the various heads of departments within the store. The purpose of the meeting is to bring the team together and to conduct a short review of the previous week's trading. More importantly, the team then start to plan the following week's activity, ensuring that the store is kept legal and the store objectives and targets are met. The store manager in one of the Bristol stores (I will call him Neil, although that is not his actual name) had just returned from attending the leadership programme and he, like many managers was keen to try out the new things that he had just learned. He was talking to one of his department heads (let's call him Bob)

'Lets look at next week's targets. Bob, I'd like you to sell one hundred cherry pies.'

Bob gulped and quietly said, 'But that's impossible boss, we only sell twenty in a good week. There is no way that we could sell one hundred in a flat week.'

Neil remembered what had happened whilst he was on his development programme and the power of asking incisive questions.

'Here goes,' he thought, 'this is my opportunity to put some of this good stuff into practice and see if it really works.'

Thinking quickly on his feet Neil asked:

'If you knew that you could sell one hundred cherry pies what would you now do?'

Bob considered the question for a moment, and then thoughtfully replied, 'I'd put some at the entrance of the store – people are more likely to pick them up from there – and I'd print off some new point-of-sale material so that people can see that they are good value and ...' Bob was starting to pick up pace with his response as the ideas started to flow more readily, ' ... and I'd use the tannoy system to put out an announcement to advertise them to our customers, oh and I'd make a bit more room for them on the fixture and put some tasters out. Customers love that, don't they? Finally I'd involve the girls down at the checkouts – they talk to the customers so there is always an opportunity for them to actively sell products.'

In less than a minute Bob had hatched a cunning plan and it was obvious to Neil from his energy and new-found state that he had bought into making the plan work. He had a challenge that he was now ready to rise to and a simple but effective plan that could support him in achieving it.

Neil was really pleased that he had been able to use an incisive question with only a moment's thought. There was nothing complicated about this, in fact he was amazed at how simple it was.

A week later the store team got together to plan for the following week and review all the good things that had happened the week before.

'A good performance last week by everyone, well done team, thanks for all of your hard work. I've also got a special acknowledgement to make; do any of you remember the challenge that was set to Bob last week? Maybe you could remind the team Bob,' suggested Neil.

'I was challenged with selling one hundred cherry pies,' replied Bob smiling.

'*Are you going to tell the team how many you actually sold?*' *asked Neil.*

'*Two hundred and one,*' *replied Bob proudly.*

'*Well done, that is a brilliant performance! I knew that you could do it,*' *said Neil, patting Bob on the back.*

Bob smiled as he was pleased to receive such public praise, but then he slowly bowed his head and looked at the floor. '*Actually it wasn't down to me, if it hadn't been for Denise on the checkout we wouldn't have achieved the target that you set.*'

'*That's great that you involved Denise to achieve your result, well done. Just one thing, please can you make sure that Denise knows what you have achieved between you? It's important that we recognise and appreciate the role that she has played. Maybe you could give her a cherry pie? I'll leave it with you to decide.*'

As soon as the meeting finished Bob sprung into action, walking onto the sales floor, he headed to the bakery department and picked up a freshly baked cherry pie. He headed down to the checkout area, waited for Denise to finish serving a customer and then walked over to her with the 99p cherry pie balanced in the palm of his hand.

'*I just wanted to say thank you for helping me last week, we smashed the target that was set, we didn't sell one hundred cherry pies, we sold just over two hundred. I know it's not a lot but please take this home and enjoy this cherry pie on me – we could not have done so well without you. Thank you.*'

Denise looked at him. Initially she was surprised that he had gone to such extremes, then her eyes started to fill with tears. '*I don't know what to say,*' *she replied.* '*That's the nicest thing that anyone has ever done for me in my ten years here.*'

This may sound like a very simple story that achieved a small operational/financial result. However, if this one story had been replicated in every one of our stores across the country this is what we might have seen:

- *an additional £216,000 being put in the tills each week*
- *an additional £11.2 million added to the sales line across the year*
- *and what that equals for the shareholder is an additional £3.4 million profit*
- *... all of that for only 99p!!*

By behaving differently, the store manager was able to achieve a result that was initially perceived to be impossible by the department manager. Neil learnt that by asking an incisive question he could engage and motivate his team towards achieving 'their' results. How likely was it that Bob would have achieved the result if Neil had told him what to do? How likely was it that Bob would be motivated to take such action again? How likely was it that doing the same things again would achieve another better result? Well, it could happen, but I'd suggest that based upon the performance that we have seen in the past it is very likely that we would see no change.

The Personal Leadership Programme gave our delegates the confidence and the opportunity to go away and behave differently. The commitment of the business to leadership gave the delegates the environment and support to make this possible. There is no rocket science involved in asking or listening or appreciating, it is all common sense. That is all that happened in this story, the application of a small amount of common sense and the confidence to behave differently.

From the day that we received the call from Neil and heard his story we started to term every good news story a 'Cherry Pie'. We were always asking people to share their own Cherry Pie stories. There were many, many more of them and people were proud to share them. Of course some Cherry Pies added much more money to the bottom line than the simple story that you have just read. We heard about buyers working with suppliers differently, finance managers treating contacts differently, stores working with the supply chain more effectively and better and quicker decisions being made. We were behaving better in meetings, which meant that everyone had the opportunity to have a say and to add value. This meant that we were listening to the good thoughts and ideas that our people had. After all, they were the ones who truly knew our business.

Next time that you think about making a measurable difference in your business, think about something nice, something gooey, smell that gorgeous smell of freshly baked sweet pastry, all brown around the edges with the sweet scent of caramelised sugar on the top. See the bright red luxurious filling gushing out of the edges of the pastry as you cut it ready to take a slice and feel excited about eating it. Be happy to share it with your friends and colleagues because Cherry Pies are good: in fact Cherry Pies can make a sustainable difference to business performance and that means that Cherry Pies are great!

Sally Pattison
Director
Ducks In A Row

The measurable results of personal leadership

Over the past 18 months, reports about wholesale energy costs have continued to make the headlines. Behind the news stories is the fact that wholesale energy prices have rocketed. The reality is that all of the major energy suppliers are facing the same volatile market and have had to increase their prices over the last few months.

It's a situation that concerns us all, especially here at British Gas Business. We supply gas to businesses throughout England, Scotland and Wales. British Gas Business is part of the Centrica Group, which also includes British Gas Retail and British Gas Services as well as operations in Europe and North America. Centrica is an organisation which has seen much change in its short existence. For instance, since 1998, British Gas Retail has become the largest supplier of domestic electricity, and grew its services business to provide care for over four million heating and kitchen appliances – major growth areas – combined with the acquisition and subsequent sale of businesses like AA and One Tel. It has always been critical to our businesses that we get close to our customers, close to our employees and offer a service that is second to none.

In 2003, in British Gas Business, our new MD moved across from another division of the business and, although we were already successful, from his new perspective he could see tremendous scope for growth. However, he could also recognise that there were many elements of behaviour and activity that were not compatible with his aims.

After a period of 12 months absorbing the way the business worked, defining a strategy and creating a set of values that would move the business forward, he decided to take some positive action.

One of our senior managers had just attended the Personal Leadership Programme and the review I then received as the HR Director captured the enthusiasm and the imagination of our MD. He felt that this might help us to generate the involvement and sense of ownership necessary to achieve the goals. In just six weeks 200 of our managers experienced the programme. Their shared journey created new behaviours and established a common language. We have always recognised that the knowledge and experience of our people is what makes us strong, so generating more open, free flowing communication that captured, shared and capitalised on the knowledge and experience of our team, was really exciting.

BGB saw results come quickly, achieving a significant, positive shift in employee engagement, absence and labour turnover statistics. In fact, employee engagement increased by 21%! One of the most significant and key measures of success for the business was the reduction in repeat customer calls, which means improved customer service and increased profitability. Profit was up by over 50% and we were the most successful division in 2005. This has been driven by the increased ownership from the front line and the recognition that they have received for the great work that they have done. One of the most important accolades for everyone in the team is what employees have said about the business. This year (2006) BGB were voted by their own employees into the *Financial Times'* 'Best Places to Work' and the *Sunday Times'* 'Best Companies to Work For'.

Such recognition should make everyone proud of the team and the step change that they have achieved. Leadership isn't just about the inspirational leader that leads this team. It's about developing everyone so that they have the ability to make the difference. Finally it's about doing the little things that give them the belief and understanding that '*they*' are the difference.

Jill Shedden
Human Resources Director
British Gas Business

■

There is enough energy at British Gas Business to power the entire United Kingdom – and that is just from the staff. You can feel the positively electric enthusiasm the moment you walk into the firm's headquarters.
FT Best Companies to Work For 2006

■

INDEX